Maan Al Saleh is a senior sales and business development consultant in IT domain since 1998, selling IT solutions to finance, government and enterprise sectors.

He is a championed driving business excellence, with core competencies in sales, marketing and account management, focused on excellent customer service delivery, profit sustainability and people agenda.

He developed a profitable business and managed key accounts.

He communicates with key stakeholders at all levels. He has proven records of accomplishments of target achievements with large deals size, and he built a strong network of contacts across all sectors in UAE.

I dedicate this book to my guardian angel and my soul mate Mrs. Rosette Gibran, who believed in me and my capabilities, she supported me emotionally and financially for this book to see the light, the light of knowledge for future generations to learn the art of selling IT systems to big companies.

Maan Al Saleh

The Art of Selling IT Technology to Large Enterprises

Austin Macauley Publishers™

LONDON • CAMBRIDGE • NEW YORK • SHARJAH

Copyright © Maan Al Saleh 2023

The right of Maan Al Saleh to be identified as author of this work has been asserted by the author in accordance with Federal Law No. (7) of UAE, Year 2002, Concerning Copyrights and Neighboring Rights.

All rights reserved. No part of this publication may be reproduced, stored in a retrieval system, or transmitted in any form or by any means, electronic, mechanical, photocopying, recording, or otherwise, without the prior permission of the publishers.

Any person who commits any unauthorized act in relation to this publication may be liable to legal prosecution and civil claims for damages.

The age group that matches the content of the books has been classified according to the age classification system issued by the Ministry of Culture and Youth.

ISBN 9789948775492 (Paperback)
ISBN 9789948775485 (E-Book)

Application Number: MC-10-01-4627908
Age Classification: E

First Published 2023
AUSTIN MACAULEY PUBLISHERS FZE
Sharjah Publishing City
P.O Box [519201]
Sharjah, UAE
www.austinmacauley.ae
+971 655 95 202

I would like to thank God who is the source of my inspiration to write this book. And special thanks to all my managers and customers who are the real mentors who taught me and guided me to be a dedicated salesman.

Table of Contents

Chapter 1   **19**

Understanding the IT Industry and the Sales Tactics   *19*

1 – Why IT Sales Training Program	19
2 – ABC Rules in IT Sales	21
3 – What Are the Unique Values of IT Sales Training for IT Sales Team?	21
4 – What Are the Unique Values of an IT Sales Training to the Companies?	22
5 – Why Sales Training for High-End Technology for High-End Organizations?	23
6 – What Is Return on Investment (ROI)?	25
7 – What Is the Total Cost of Ownership (TCO)?	26
8 – What Are the IT Sales Tactics?	27
9 – What Is an IT Solution Selling?	28
10 – What Is an IT Value Selling?	29
11 – What Is an IT Consultative Selling?	30
12 – What Is an IT Relationship Selling?	32

13 – What Is an IT Upselling?	33
14 – What Is an IT Cross-Selling?	34
15 – What Are the Cons of an IT Sales?	34
16 – How to Use Emotional Intelligence as an IT Salesperson?	35
17 – What Are the Emotional intelligence Tactics in IT Domain?	36
18 – What Is the Compelling Event in IT Sales Domain?	38
19 – What Is the Persuasive Language?	39
20 – How to Create Sales Goals in IT Domain?	40
21 – What Is the IT Sales Goals?	42
22 – Creating Value in IT Sales Domain.	43
23 – Tips and Tricks for Success in IT Domain Sales?	44

Chapter 2 — **47**

Building a Sales Champion — *47*

1 – How to Be a Champion IT Salesman?	47
2 – What Kind of Spirit the IT Salesman Should Have?	48
3 – How to Handle the Cold Calls as an IT Salesperson?	49
4 – How to Master the Time Management of the IT Salesman?	50

5 – What Are the Handling Objections Skills for an IT Salesperson? 51

6 – How to Avoid the Violent Objection in IT Sales Domain? 52

7 – How to Handle the Rejection as an IT Salesperson? 53

8 – How to Handle the Pressure as an IT Salesperson? 54

9 – How to Handle the Success as an IT Salesperson? 55

10 – How to Handle the Sales Manager as an IT Salesperson? 56

11 – How to Handle the C Level as an IT Salesperson? 57

12 – How to Handle the Customer Presentation as an IT Salesperson? 58

13 – How to Handle the Preparation of the Customer POC as an IT Salesperson? 59

14 – How to Handle the Foxes at the Customer Site as an IT Salesperson? 60

15 – How to Find Out the Foxes at the Customer Site as an IT Salesperson? 61

16 – How to Earn the Trust of the Foxes at the Customer Site as an IT Salesperson? 62

17 – What Are the Personal and the Organizational Agenda of the Foxes? 63

18 – How to Find Out the Personal Agenda of the Foxes at the Customer Site as an IT Salesperson? 64

19 – How to Find Out the Organization Agenda of the Foxes? 65

20 – How to Convert a Fox to Coach? 66

21 – What Is a Sales Pitch? 67

22 – What Is the Best Sales Pitch in IT Domain? 68

23 – How to Ask an Open-Ended Question to the Foxes at the Customer Site? 69

24 – How to Use Positive Body Language as an IT Salesperson? 70

25 – What Is the Leadership Skills? 71

26 – What Are the Descriptions of an IT Businessman? 72

27 – What Is Hunter Salesman and Farmer Salesman? 74

28 – How to Be Hunter Salesman? 75

29 – How to Be a Farmer Salesman? 76

Chapter 3 78

How to Handle the RIGHT Customer? 78

1 – How to Sharp the Ax Before Facing a Customer in IT Domain? 78

2 – How to Sharpen My Ax Every Morning? 79

3 – How to Motivate Myself Every Morning? 80

4 – How to Plan Your Day as an IT Salesman? 82

5 – Engorging Statements for IT Salesmen. 83
6 – How to Treat an Existing Customer? 85
7 – How to Treat a New Customer? 85
8 – How to Be a Positive Thinker? 86
9 – What Are the Main Values to have an Emotional Intelligent Behavior? 88
10 – How to Learn Emotional Intelligent Behavior? 89
11 – What to Do to Have an Emotional Intelligent Behavior? 90
12 – How to Sell Value to Your Customer? 91
13 – How to Perfect Your IT Sales Pitch Introduction with Your Customer? 93
14 – How to Make a Successful Sales Call in IT Domain? 94
15 – What Are the Tips for Making a Successful Sales Call in IT Domain? 95
16 – What Are the Descriptions of an IT Customer? 97
17 – Customer Relationship Management (CRM) System 98
18 – Consultative Selling 99
19 – What Are the Open-Ended Questions in IT Domain? 100
20 – How to Sell Value in IT Domain? 101
21 – How to Present Your Solution to Your Customer? 102

22 – How to Keep the Deal Moving with Your Customer? 104
23 – Who Is the Right Customer to an IT Salesman? 105
24 – How to Evaluate the Customer in IT Domain? 106
25 – How to Build a Relationship with Your Customer? 108
26 – How to Build a Long-Term Relationship with Customer in IT Domain? 109
27 – What Is the Hidden Agenda in IT Business? 110
28 – What Is the Organizational Agenda of the Customer in IT Domain? 111
29 – What Is the Personal Agenda of the Customer in IT Domain? 112
30 – How to Do a First Meeting with a Prospect in IT Domain? 114
31 – What Types of Objections Customers Have in IT Domain? 115
32 – How to Handle Customer's Rejection as an IT Salesman? 116
33 – How to Respond to Customer's Objections in IT Domain? 117
34 – What Are the Techniques for Handling Customer's Objections in IT Domain? 118
35 – What Are the Decision-Making Criteria? 120
36 – Who Are the Decision-Influencers at the Customer Site in IT Domain? 121

37 – Who Are the Decision-Makers at the Customer Site in IT Domain? 122

Chapter 4 — 124

Opportunity's Sales Cycle — *124*

1 – Sales Process 124
2 – Sales Funnel 125
3 – Sales Cycle 127
4 – Lead Generation 129
5 – How to Generate a Lead? 130
6 – Here Are Some Tips for Making a Successful Sales Call to Your Lead: 132
7 – What Are the Active Listening Techniques? 133
8 – How to Convert Leads to Prospects? 134
9 – How to Evaluate the Prospects? 135
10 – How to Convert Prospects into Opportunity? 137
11 – How to Evaluate the Opportunity? 138
12 – How to Move the Opportunity into the Closing? 140
13 – What Is the Opportunity Sales Cycle Process? 141
14 – Don't Do the Common Mistakes During the Sales Process 143
15 – What Is the Sales Opportunity Assessment Tool? 144
16 – What Are the Sales Opportunity Evaluation Criteria? 145

17 – Negotiation Strategies in IT Domain	146
18 – What Are the Effective Communication and Negotiation Skills?	148
19 – What Are the Negotiation Terminologies?	149
20 – What Is the Decoy in IT Negotiation Domain?	150
21 – How to Negotiate Effectively in IT Domain?	152
22 – What Is the Preparation Before Negotiation in IT Domain?	153
23 – What Is Win-Win Negotiation Strategy?	154
24 – What Are the Negotiation Strategies in IT Domain?	155
25 – What Are the Negotiation Techniques?	156
26 – What Are the Negotiation Tactics?	158
27 – How to Negotiate Positively?	159
28 – What Are the Competition Terminologies?	160
29 – What Is the Competitive Analysis?	161
Competitive Analysis	162
30 – What Is the SWOT Analysis?	163
SWOT Analysis	164
31 – How to Handle the Competition as an IT Salesperson?	164
32 – What Are the Competition Strategies?	165
33 – How to Attack Competition?	167
34 – How to Team-Up with My Competitor?	168
35 – What Are the Competition Techniques?	170
36 – Changing the Ground Rules?	171

37 – Closing Deal in IT Domain:	173
38 – What Are the Closing Techniques?	174
39 – What Are the Closing Deal Terminologies?	176
40 – What Are the Closing Skills for an IT Salesperson?	177
41 – Closing Mistakes	178

Chapter 5 — **180**

IT Domain Terminologies — *180*

1 – What Are the IT Business Terminologies?	180
2 – What Are the IT Finance Terminologies?	181
3 – What Are the IT Technical Terminologies?	182
4 – What Are the IT Infrastructure Terminologies?	184
5 – What Are the IT Application Terminologies?	185
6 – What Are the IT Managed Services Terminologies?	186
7 – What Are the IT Consultancy Services Terminologies?	188
8 – What Are the Cyber Security Terminologies?	189
9 – What Are the IT Cloud Terminologies?	190
10 – What Are the IT Business Continuity Terminologies?	192
11 – What Are the IT NOC Terminologies?	193
12 – What Are the IT SOC Terminologies?	195
13 – What Are the IT Data Centre Terminologies?	196
14 – What Are the IT DR Terminologies?	197

15 – What Are the IT Production site Terminologies?	198
16 – What Are the IT HCI Terminologies?	200
17 – What Are the IT Storage Terminologies?	201
18 – What Are the IT Compute Terminologies?	202
19 – What Are the IT AI Terminologies?	203
20 – What Are the IT BI Terminologies?	204
21 – What Are the IT Support Service Terminologies?	205
22 – What Are the IT Network Terminologies?	206

Chapter 1

Understanding the IT Industry and the Sales Tactics

1 – Why IT Sales Training Program

An IT sales training program typically involves a series of steps designed to help sales professionals develop the skills and knowledge they need to be successful in the IT industry. Here are the key steps that are often included in an IT sales training program:

1. Overview of the IT industry: This step typically involves providing an overview of the IT industry, including key players, trends, and challenges. This helps sales professionals understand the broader context in which they will be operating.
2. Product training: In this step, sales professionals are trained on the specific products or solutions they will be selling. This includes learning about the features and benefits of the products, as well as how to demo and present them to potential customers.

3. Sales process training: Sales professionals are also trained on the specific sales process that they will be following. This includes understanding how to identify potential leads, develop relationships with customers, and close sales.
4. Communication skills training: Effective communication is a crucial part of the sales process. Training programs often include sessions on how to effectively communicate with potential customers, including how to listen and ask effective questions
5. Closing techniques training: Closing a sale is the final step in the sales process. Sales training programs often include training on various closing techniques, such as the "assumptive close" and the "alternative close."
6. Role-playing and practice: Finally, many sales training programs include opportunities for sales professionals to practice their skills through role-playing exercises and mock sales calls. This helps them build confidence and hone their skills in a realistic setting.

Overall, an IT sales training program is designed to help sales professionals develop the skills and knowledge they need to effectively sell IT products and solutions to potential customers.

2 – ABC Rules in IT Sales

The ABC rules in IT sales refer to the practice of prioritizing potential customers or leads based on their potential value to the company.

"A" leads are high-value, highly qualified potential customers that are likely to result in a large sale or a long-term business relationship.

"B" leads are of medium value and may require more effort to close the sale.

"C" leads are lower value and may not be worth pursuing.

The ABC method helps sales teams prioritize their efforts and focus on the most valuable opportunities.

3 – What Are the Unique Values of IT Sales Training for IT Sales Team?

IT sales training can help individuals develop a range of valuable skills, including:

1. Knowledge of technology: IT sales training can help individuals learn about different types of technology, as well as how different technologies can be used in different business contexts.
2. Strong communication skills: IT sales training can help individuals develop the ability to clearly articulate the benefits and value of the products or services they are selling. They can also learn how to explain technical concepts in a way that is easy for non-technical people to understand.
3. Persistence and determination: IT sales training can help individuals learn how to handle rejection and

continue to pursue leads and opportunities, even in the face of setbacks.
4. Ability to build relationships: IT sales training can help individuals learn how to build strong relationships with customers, partners, and other stakeholders. This includes the ability to listen to their needs and find ways to meet them.
5. Adaptability: IT sales training can help individuals learn how to adapt to changing market conditions and customer needs, as well as be open to learning about new technologies and products.
6. Business acumen: IT sales training can help individuals develop a good understanding of business principles and learn how to identify opportunities for technology to solve business problems.

4 – What Are the Unique Values of an IT Sales Training to the Companies?

There are several unique values that IT sales training can bring to companies:

1. Improved sales performance: With IT sales training, companies can help their sales team members improve their knowledge of technology, communication skills, and other key sales skills. This can lead to increased sales and revenue.
2. Enhanced customer satisfaction: With IT sales training, companies can help their sales team members better understand customer needs and find

ways to meet them. This can lead to improved customer satisfaction and loyalty.
3. Greater efficiency: With IT sales training, companies can help their sales team members streamline their sales processes and work more efficiently. This can lead to increased productivity and cost savings.
4. Improved competitiveness: With IT sales training, companies can help their sales team members stay up to date on the latest technologies and best practices, which can give them a competitive advantage in the market.
5. Greater employee retention: By investing in the professional development of their sales team, companies can help employees feel more valued and engaged. This can lead to lower turnover and improved retention.

Enhanced company reputation: By providing IT sales training to their employees, companies can demonstrate their commit.

5 – Why Sales Training for High-End Technology for High-End Organizations?

Sales training for high-end technology for high-end organizations typically focuses on helping sales professionals understand and effectively sell complex, high-value solutions to large enterprise customers. Some key elements of this type of training may include:

1. Product knowledge: Sales professionals will receive detailed training on the technical features and capabilities of the high-end technology products and solutions they will be selling.
2. Industry knowledge: Sales professionals will also receive training on the industry or industries that their products and solutions are intended for, so they can understand the specific needs and challenges that their customers face.
3. Solution selling: Sales professionals will be trained on how to sell solutions, not just products. This means understanding the customer's business needs and pain points and presenting solutions that address those needs.
4. Value proposition: Sales professionals will be trained on how to communicate the value that their products and solutions can bring to customers. This includes understanding the return on investment (ROI) and total cost of ownership (TCO) of the solution and how it can improve business outcomes.
5. Sales process: Sales professionals will be trained on a specific sales process that is tailored to the high-end technology market. This may include steps such as identifying key decision-makers, building relationships, and developing customized presentations and proposals.
6. Account management: Sales professionals will be trained on how to manage large and complex customer accounts, including how to identify and target new opportunities within existing accounts.

7. Negotiation and closing: Sales professionals will be trained on how to effectively negotiate and close deals with large enterprise customers.
8. Product demonstration: Sales professionals will be trained on how to demonstrate the product or solution and how to handle objections effectively.
9. Post-sales support: Sales professionals will be trained on how to provide post-sales support, including how to handle any issues that may arise and how to ensure customer satisfaction.

Overall, the goal of this type of sales training is to equip sales professionals with the knowledge, skills, and tools they need to effectively sell high-end technology solutions to large enterprise customers, close deals and grow the business.

6 – What Is Return on Investment (ROI)?

Return on Investment (ROI) is a financial metric used to evaluate the profitability of an investment. It is the ratio of the net gain or loss of an investment relative to its initial cost.

The formula for calculating ROI is: ROI = (Net Gain or Loss from Investment / Cost of Investment) X 100%. The net gain or loss from the investment is calculated by subtracting the cost of the investment from the revenue generated from the investment. For example, if you invested $10,000 in a stock and sold it for $12,000, your net gain from the investment would be $2,000. If your initial cost of investment was $10,000, your ROI would be: ROI = ($2,000 / $10,000) x 100% = 20%

This means that your investment generated a 20% return relative to its initial cost.

ROI is an important metric for evaluating the efficiency and profitability of an investment. It is commonly used by investors, business owners, and financial analysts to compare the performance of different investments and to make informed investment decisions.

7 – What Is the Total Cost of Ownership (TCO)?

Total Cost of Ownership (TCO) is a financial estimate that attempts to determine all of the costs associated with a product or service over its entire life cycle. It includes not only the initial purchase price of the product or service, but also the costs of operating, maintaining, and disposing of it.

TCO typically includes the following costs:

1. Initial purchase price: The cost of the product or service at the time of purchase.
2. Operating costs: These include costs such as energy consumption, maintenance, and repairs.
3. Administrative costs: These include costs associated with managing the product or service, such as training, documentation, and licensing.
4. Upgrade and replacement costs: These include costs associated with upgrading or replacing the product or service.
5. Disposal costs: These include costs associated with disposing of the product or service at the end of its life cycle.

6. Opportunity costs: These include the costs of not having the product or service, such as lost productivity, lost revenue, and increased risk.

The goal of TCO analysis is to provide a comprehensive view of the costs associated with a product or service and to help organizations make informed decisions about which products or services will be the most cost-effective over the long term.

TCO is used in various industries and it's particularly relevant in IT, where the costs associated with technology products and services can be significant and complex. By understanding the total cost of ownership, organizations can more accurately predict and manage the costs of IT investments over time.

8 – What Are the IT Sales Tactics?

IT sales tactics are specific strategies and techniques used to sell technology products and services. Here are some common tactics used in IT sales:

1. Solution selling: Focusing on the customer's needs and how the product or service can solve their problems.
2. Value selling: Emphasizing the value and benefits of the product or service to the customer.
3. Consultative selling: Acting as a consultant, providing advice and expertise to the customer.

4. Relationship selling: Building a long-term relationship with the customer based on trust and mutual benefit.
5. Upselling: Offering additional products or services that complement the customer's current purchase.
6. Cross-selling: Offering complementary products or services that may be of interest to the customer.
7. Lead generation: Identifying and qualifying potential customers through various marketing and sales techniques.
8. Marketing automation: Using tools and software to automate and streamline marketing and sales processes.
9. Digital selling: Using online and digital platforms to reach and engage with customers.
10. Sales enablement: Providing sales teams with the training, tools, and resources they need to be successful.

It is important to note that, just like any sales process, IT sales require a good understanding of the customer's needs and pain points, as well as the features and benefits of the product or service being sold. Also, building a trustful relationship with the customer, and following up after the sale are crucial steps in the IT sales process.

9 – What Is an IT Solution Selling?

Solution selling is a sales strategy that focuses on the customer's needs and how the product or service can solve their problems. It is a process of understanding the customer's business and identifying the problems they are facing, then presenting a tailored solution that addresses those problems. It is a consultative approach that aims to build a long-term relationship with the customer based on trust and mutual benefit.

The IT solution selling process typically includes the following steps:

1. Identifying and qualifying potential customers
2. Researching and understanding the customer's business and needs
3. Presenting a tailored solution that addresses the customer's specific problems
4. Demonstrating the value and benefits of the solution
5. Handling objections and addressing concerns
6. Closing the sale and providing ongoing support

Solution selling is particularly effective in the IT industry, where products and services can be complex and require a high level of technical expertise. By demonstrating a deep understanding of the customer's needs and providing a tailored solution, IT solution sellers can differentiate themselves from competitors and build trust with customers.

10 – What Is an IT Value Selling?

IT value selling is a sales strategy that emphasizes the value and benefits of the product or service to the customer. It focuses on how the product or service can help the customer improve their business operations, increase efficiency, and reduce costs. Instead of just highlighting the features of the product or service, the IT value seller will show how those features align with the customer's specific needs and goals.

The IT value selling process typically includes the following steps:

1. Identifying and qualifying potential customers
2. Researching and understanding the customer's business and needs
3. Identifying the customer's pain points and challenges
4. Communicating the value proposition of the product or service
5. Demonstrating how the product or service addresses the customer's specific needs and goals
6. Handling objections and addressing concerns
7. Closing the sale and providing ongoing support

IT value selling is particularly useful in the IT industry where products and services can be complex and the customer may not be aware of the full potential of the product or service. By emphasizing the value and benefits of the product or service, IT value sellers can help customers understand how the product or service can improve their business operations and make their lives easier.

11 – What Is an IT Consultative Selling?

IT consultative selling is a sales strategy where the salesperson acts as a consultant, providing advice and expertise to the customer. The focus is on understanding the customer's business and unique needs, and providing a tailored solution that addresses those needs.

The IT consultative selling process typically includes the following steps:

1. Identifying and qualifying potential customers
2. Researching and understanding the customer's business and needs
3. Identifying the customer's pain points and challenges
4. Providing expert advice and recommendations on how to address those challenges
5. Presenting a tailored solution that addresses the customer's specific needs
6. Demonstrating the value and benefits of the solution
7. Handling objections and addressing concerns.
8. Building trust and rapport with the customer.
9. Asking open-ended questions to gather information and uncover the customer's needs.
10. Continuously following up and checking in with the customer to ensure they are satisfied with your solution and to identify any additional needs.
11. Closing the sale and providing ongoing support.

IT consultative selling is particularly effective in the IT industry, where products and services can be complex and require a high level of technical expertise. By acting as a consultant and providing expert advice, IT consultative sellers can build trust with customers and differentiate themselves from competitors. It is also a good approach to build long-term relationships with customers, as the customers will rely on the seller's expertise in the future.

12 – What Is an IT Relationship Selling?

IT relationship selling is a sales strategy that focuses on building long-term relationships with customers based on trust and mutual benefit. The goal is to become a trusted advisor to the customer, providing ongoing support and guidance to help them achieve their business goals.

The IT relationship selling process typically includes the following steps:

1. Identifying and qualifying potential customers
2. Building trust and rapport with the customer
3. Understanding the customer's business and needs
4. Providing ongoing support and guidance to help the customer achieve their goals
5. Continuously monitoring the customer's needs and updating the solution accordingly
6. Providing customer service and addressing concerns
7. Upselling and cross-selling additional products and services
8. Building a loyal customer base.

IT relationship selling is particularly useful in the IT industry, where customers may have ongoing needs and require ongoing support. By building a long-term relationship with the customer, IT relationship sellers can ensure that they are the go-to provider for the customer's future needs. This approach is also beneficial for the seller as it can lead to repeat sales and positive word-of-mouth recommendations.

13 – What Is an IT Upselling?

IT upselling is a sales tactic where the salesperson offers additional products or services that complement the customer's current purchase. The goal is to increase the value of the sale by offering the customer additional products or services that they may need or find useful.

For example, if a customer is buying a new computer, the salesperson may offer an extended warranty, a software package, or additional memory and storage.

The IT upselling process typically includes the following steps:

1. Identifying the customer's needs and interests
2. Offering additional products or services that complement the customer's current purchase
3. Demonstrating the value and benefits of the additional products or services
4. Handling objections and addressing concerns
5. Closing the sale and providing ongoing support

IT upselling can be a useful tactic for increasing revenue and building customer loyalty. By offering additional products or services that meet the customer's needs, the salesperson can provide value to the customer and make the purchase more beneficial for them. However, it's important to make sure that the upsell is relevant and provides value to the customer, not just an attempt to increase the sale without considering the customer's needs.

14 – What Is an IT Cross-Selling?

Cross-selling in IT refers to the practice of promoting and selling additional products or services to existing customers. This can be done through upselling (offering a more advanced or expensive version of a product or service that a customer is already using) or by offering complementary products or services that would enhance the customer's current usage of the product or service they have already purchased. The goal of cross-selling is to increase revenue and customer satisfaction by providing customers with additional solutions that meet their needs.

15 – What Are the Cons of an IT Sales?

1. High pressure: IT sales can be a high-pressure job, with tight deadlines and targets that must be met. This can be stressful and challenging for some people.
2. Constant learning: The IT industry is constantly changing and evolving, so an IT salesperson needs to stay up to date with the latest products, services, and trends. This requires a significant time commitment to learning and training.
3. Rejection: IT salespeople may face rejection on a regular basis, as potential customers may not be interested in the products or services being offered.
4. Long working hours: IT salespeople may be required to put in long hours, including evenings and weekends, in order to meet deadlines and close deals.

5. Competition: There can be a high level of competition in the IT sales industry, which can make it difficult to win new business.
6. Requires travel: IT salespeople may be required to travel to meet with potential customers and partners, which can be time-consuming and tiring.
7. Technical Knowledge: IT salespeople are expected to have a good understanding of the technical aspects of the products they are selling and the services they are offering. This may be a challenge for some people.
8. Uncertainty: IT Salespeople may face uncertainty in their work, as the market conditions, customer needs, and competition are always changing.
9. Limited autonomy: IT Salespeople may have limited autonomy in terms of what they can offer to customers and how they can customize solutions.

16 – How to Use Emotional Intelligence as an IT Salesperson?

Emotional intelligence (EI) is the ability to recognize and understand your own emotions, as well as the emotions of others. As an IT salesperson, developing your EI can help you build better relationships with clients and close more deals. Here are a few tips for using emotional intelligence as an IT salesperson:

1. Practice active listening: Pay attention to what clients are saying and try to understand their emotions and needs.

2. Show empathy: Try to put yourself in the client's shoes and show that you understand their feelings and concerns.
3. Manage your own emotions: Don't let your own emotions get in the way of the sales process. Stay positive and focused, even if the client is upset or difficult to work with.
4. Use nonverbal cues: Pay attention to the nonverbal cues of clients, such as their body language and tone of voice, to better understand their emotions.

By developing your emotional intelligence, you can build stronger relationships with clients and be more effective in your sales role.

17 – What Are the Emotional intelligence Tactics in IT Domain?

Emotional intelligence is an important skill for salespeople in any industry, including IT sales. Here are some emotional intelligence tactics that can be useful for IT sales professionals:

1. Empathy: One of the most important emotional intelligence tactics is the ability to empathize with customers. Empathy involves understanding the customer's perspective, emotions, and needs. By demonstrating empathy, IT salespeople can build rapport and trust with their customers, which can be crucial in building long-term relationships.

2. Active listening: Active listening is another critical tactic for building emotional intelligence in IT sales. By listening carefully to customers and paying attention to their body language and tone of voice, salespeople can better understand their needs and emotions. This can help them tailor their approach and better address the customer's concerns.
3. Positive attitude: Maintaining a positive attitude is another important tactic for building emotional intelligence in IT sales. By maintaining a positive outlook, salespeople can help customers feel more confident in their product or service, and more receptive to their message.
4. Adaptability: IT sales professionals need to be adaptable in order to be effective. By being flexible and willing to adapt their approach to different customers and situations, salespeople can demonstrate emotional intelligence and build stronger relationships with customers.
5. Self-awareness: Being self-aware is another important tactic for building emotional intelligence in IT sales. By understanding their own emotions and tendencies, salespeople can better manage their reactions to customers and situations. This can help them avoid negative interactions and build more positive relationships.
6. Effective communication: Effective communication is a key component of emotional intelligence in IT sales. By communicating clearly and effectively, salespeople can avoid misunderstandings and build stronger relationships with customers.

Overall, emotional intelligence is an important skill for IT sales professionals, as it can help them better understand and connect with their customers, build stronger relationships, and ultimately drive more sales.

18 – What Is the Compelling Event in IT Sales Domain?

A compelling event in the IT Sales domain refers to a specific circumstance or situation that creates a sense of urgency for a potential customer to purchase a product or service. This event serves as a trigger that motivates the customer to take action and make a purchase, and it is often tied to a business need or problem that needs to be addressed.

Some examples of compelling events in the IT Sales domain may include:

End of life of a product or software: When a product or software reaches its end of life, it is no longer supported or updated by the vendor. This can create a sense of urgency for customers to find a replacement to avoid potential security risks or other issues.

New product launch: The introduction of a new product or service that addresses a specific need or provides a unique advantage can create a compelling event for customers to make a purchase.

Change in business requirements: If a business undergoes a change in operations or strategy, they may need to purchase new IT solutions to support these changes.

Security breach or data loss: A security breach or data loss can create a sense of urgency for customers to invest in new

IT solutions to improve their security posture and prevent future incidents.

Regulatory changes: Changes in industry regulations or compliance requirements may create a compelling event for customers to purchase new IT solutions to ensure they remain compliant.

Identifying the compelling event that is driving a customer's decision to purchase can help IT sales professionals tailor their messaging and offerings to better meet the customer's needs and increase their chances of closing the sale.

19 – What Is the Persuasive Language?

Persuasive language is language that is used to convince or influence someone to take a particular action, adopt a certain viewpoint, or believe in a particular idea. It is used in various contexts, including advertising, marketing, sales, politics, and even everyday conversations.

Some common techniques used in persuasive language include:

1. Emotional appeals: Using words and phrases that evoke strong emotions, such as fear, excitement, happiness, or anger, to influence the listener's opinion.
2. Repetition: Repeating key words, phrases, or ideas to reinforce their importance and increase their impact on the listener.
3. Power words: Using words that have a strong emotional or intellectual impact, such as "amazing,"

"incredible," or "proven," to capture the listener's attention and persuade them to take action.
4. Social proof: Using testimonials, statistics, or other evidence to show that others have successfully used the product or service and gained benefits from it.
5. Authority: Citing expert opinions, credentials, or endorsements to build trust and credibility with the listener.
6. Call to action: Encouraging the listener to take a specific action, such as making a purchase or signing up for a service, by using clear and direct language.

Overall, persuasive language is an effective tool for influencing others, but it should be used ethically and responsibly. It's important to be honest, clear, and respectful in communication and to avoid using manipulative or deceitful tactics.

20 – How to Create Sales Goals in IT Domain?

Creating sales goals in the IT domain requires a clear understanding of the market, the products or services being offered, and the target customers. Here are some steps to consider when creating sales goals:

1. Conduct market research: Understand the market trends, competition, and customer needs in the IT domain.

2. Identify target customers: Identify the types of customers who are most likely to purchase the products or services being offered.
3. Set specific, measurable, and achievable goals: Set clear and specific goals for the sales team, such as the number of new customers acquired, revenue generated, or deals closed.
4. Establish a timeline: Set a realistic timeline for achieving the sales goals, such as a specific date or quarter.
5. Set performance metrics: Establish performance metrics to measure the progress of the sales team, such as the number of leads generated, the close rate, or the average deal size.
6. Prioritize goals: Prioritize the goals based on their importance and the resources required to achieve them.
7. Communicate the goals: Clearly communicate the goals to the sales team and provide them with the necessary resources and support to achieve them.
8. Monitor progress: Regularly monitor the progress of the sales team against the goals and make adjustments as necessary.
9. Encourage teamwork: Encourage teamwork and collaboration among the sales team to achieve the goals.
10. Reward success: Recognize and reward the sales team for achieving the goals, which will help to motivate them to achieve even more in the future.

21 – What Is the IT Sales Goals?

IT sales goals refer to the objectives and targets set by a company or sales team in the IT industry. These goals can include:

1. Revenue: Generating a specific amount of revenue from IT sales.
2. New business: Acquiring a specific number of new customers or accounts.
3. Repeat business: Generating repeat business from existing customers.
4. Market share: Increasing market share in a specific geographic region or industry segment.
5. Product or service adoption: Increasing the adoption and usage of a specific product or service.
6. Cross-selling: Identifying and closing sales opportunities for complementary products or services.
7. Sales pipeline: Building and maintaining a strong sales pipeline by consistently identifying and qualifying new sales opportunities.
8. Sales team performance: Setting goals for the performance of the sales team, such as the number of sales calls made, presentations given, or deals closed.
9. Sales process optimization: Optimizing the sales process to increase efficiency and close more deals.
10. Cost of sales: reducing the cost of sales as a percentage of revenue.

These goals will vary based on the company's specific needs and objectives, but they all ultimately aim to drive revenue and growth for the organization.

22 – Creating Value in IT Sales Domain.

Creating value in IT sales domain involves demonstrating to potential customers that your product or service can help them achieve their goals or solve their problems in a way that is both effective and cost-efficient. Here are some strategies to consider:

1. Focus on the customer's needs: Start by understanding the customer's specific needs, challenges, and pain points. This will help you tailor your sales approach and offer solutions that meet their unique requirements.
2. Highlight the benefits: Emphasize the specific benefits that your product or service can offer to the customer. This could include increased efficiency, improved productivity, cost savings, or other advantages.
3. Demonstrate ROI: Use data and case studies to demonstrate the return on investment (ROI) that the customer can expect from your product or service. This can help to build confidence and demonstrate the value of your offering.
4. Provide customized solutions: Tailor your offering to the specific needs and requirements of the customer. This could involve customizing the product or service

to fit their specific needs, or providing additional support or training to help them achieve their goals.
5. Focus on long-term relationships: Emphasize the importance of building a long-term relationship with the customer, and offer ongoing support and consultation to help them achieve their goals over time.

By focusing on the customer's needs, highlighting the benefits, demonstrating ROI, providing customized solutions, and focusing on long-term relationships, you can effectively create value in IT sales domain and position your product or service for success.

23 – Tips and Tricks for Success in IT Domain Sales?

Here are a few tips and tricks for success in IT domain sales:

1. Understand the market: Understand the IT market and stay up-to-date with the latest trends and technologies.
2. Understand your product: Understand your IT products or services and be able to demonstrate the value they can bring to customers.
3. Build relationships: Build relationships with customers and establish trust to increase the likelihood of future sales opportunities.

4. Use a consultative approach: Approach sales calls as consultations, ask questions and understand the customer's needs and tailor your pitch accordingly.
5. Use technology: Use technology such as customer relationship management systems to track customer interactions and sales activities, and automate repetitive tasks and processes.
6. Continuously improve: Continuously improve and adapt your sales approach by testing new methods, measuring results and making adjustments accordingly.
7. Personalize the pitch: Tailor the sales pitch to the customer's specific needs and pain points.
8. Be solutions oriented: Offer solutions that address the customer's specific needs and pain points.
9. Be prepared to handle objections: Anticipate and be prepared to address any objections or concerns the customer may have.
10. Follow up: Follow up with the customer after the call to answer any remaining questions and solidify the sale.
11. Build a strong team: Build a strong team of sales and customer service professionals who are knowledgeable about your IT products or services and have a consultative approach to selling.
12. Use forecasting: Use forecasting tools to predict future sales based on the pipeline and historical data, which can help with resource planning and budgeting.
13. Measure the effectiveness of your strategies: Measure the effectiveness of your strategies such as lead

generation, closing, and follow-up and optimize them accordingly.

Chapter 2

Building a Sales Champion

1 – How to Be a Champion IT Salesman?

Being a successful IT salesman requires a combination of knowledge, skills, and attributes. Some key strategies for becoming a champion IT salesman include:

Develop a deep understanding of the products and services you are selling: It is important to have a thorough knowledge of the technical details of the products and services you are selling, as well as an understanding of the industry and market trends.

1. Build strong relationships with customers: Building strong relationships with customers is key to understanding their needs and providing them with solutions that will meet those needs.
2. Communicate effectively: Being able to effectively communicate the value of your products and services to customers is crucial. It's important to be able to explain technical details in a clear and simple way,

and to be able to answer any questions customers may have.
3. Be persistent: Sales can be a challenging and competitive field, so it's important to be persistent in reaching out to potential customers and following up with leads.
4. Continuously improve your skills: Stay current with the industry and market trends and be open to learning new technologies and products. Network with other sales professionals, learn from their experiences and take the best practices to improve your own performance.
5. Be a problem solver: Instead of just trying to sell a product, try to understand the customers pain points and present them with a solution that addresses their needs.
6. Be ethical and Honest: Always be transparent with your clients, be upfront about what you can and cannot do, and avoid making false claims or promises.

By developing and honing these skills, you can become a champion IT salesman and be successful in selling IT products and services.

2 – What Kind of Spirit the IT Salesman Should Have?

An IT salesperson should have a positive, professional, and customer-focused attitude. Some specific qualities that may be helpful for an IT salesperson to have include:

1. Enthusiasm: Show a genuine interest in the products or services you are selling, and be excited to share that with your customers.
2. Confidence: Believe in the value of what you are offering, and be able to communicate that to your customers in a way that inspires confidence.
3. Problem-solving skills: Be able to identify and address any challenges or objections that a customer may have, and find creative solutions to meet their needs.
4. Adaptability: Be open to learning about new products and technologies, and be able to adapt your sales approach to different customers and situations.
5. Persistence: Be willing to work hard and follow up with leads and customers to close sales.

By cultivating these qualities, you can develop the spirit of a successful IT salesperson.

3 – How to Handle the Cold Calls as an IT Salesperson?

Cold calling can be an effective way to reach potential customers, but it can also be challenging and require a certain level of skill and finesse. Here are a few strategies for handling cold calls as an IT salesperson:

1. Prepare: Research the company or individual you are calling and have a clear understanding of what you are selling and how it can benefit the customer.

2. Be respectful: Remember that the person you are calling may not have asked to speak with you, so it is important to be respectful of their time and to get to the point quickly.
3. Use a script: Having a script or outline of what you want to say can help you stay focused and organized during the call.
4. Listen: Pay attention to the customer's needs and concerns, and be prepared to address any objections they may have.
5. Follow up: If the customer is not interested in your product or service, follow up with a thank-you note or email and keep them in mind for future opportunities.

By following these strategies, you can help make cold calling a more successful and effective part of your sales strategy.

4 – How to Master the Time Management of the IT Salesman?

1. Set clear goals and priorities: Identify the most important tasks that need to be accomplished and prioritize them.
2. Create a schedule: Plan your day and week in advance, including time for meetings, sales calls, and administrative tasks.
3. Use a CRM: A customer relationship management (CRM) system can help you keep track of leads,

contacts, and sales opportunities, and allow you to plan and organize your sales activities more effectively.
4. Minimize distractions: Identify the things that distract you and find ways to minimize or eliminate them.
5. Learn to say no: It's important to learn how to say no to tasks or requests that are not important or do not align with your goals.
6. Delegate: When possible, delegate tasks to others on your team to free up your time for more important activities.
7. Take regular breaks: Taking regular breaks can help you stay focused and avoid burnout.
8. Review and Reflect: At the end of the day, review what you accomplished and reflect on how you can do better the next day.

It's important to note that time management is a skill that takes practice and discipline to master. It's also important to be flexible and to adjust your approach as needed.

5 – What Are the Handling Objections Skills for an IT Salesperson?

As an IT salesperson, you will inevitably encounter objections from customers during the sales process. Handling objections effectively is an important skill to master in order to persuade customers to make a purchase. Some key strategies for handling objections include:

1. Listen actively: Make sure to fully understand the customer's objections, and ask clarifying questions if necessary.
2. Acknowledge the objection: Validate the customer's concerns and show that you understand their perspective.
3. Respond to the objection: Address the customer's concerns and provide information that addresses their objections.
4. Ask for the sale: Once you have addressed the customer's objections, ask for the sale in a confident and persuasive manner.

By following these steps, IT salespeople can effectively handle objections and persuade customers to make a purchase.

6 – How to Avoid the Violent Objection in IT Sales Domain?

Avoiding violent objections in IT sales requires a proactive approach to addressing potential sources of conflict and resistance before they become major issues. Here are some strategies that can help:

1. Build rapport: Establishing a positive relationship with the prospect is key to avoiding violent objections. Take the time to get to know the person and understand their needs, goals, and concerns.
2. Listen carefully: Listen to the prospect's objections and concerns, and address them directly and honestly.

Repeat their concerns back to them to ensure that you understand them correctly and ask questions to gather more information if necessary.
3. Communicate clearly: Use clear and simple language, avoid jargon or technical terms that the prospect may not understand, and focus on the benefits of your product or service rather than its features.
4. Show value: Emphasize the value of your product or service and how it can solve the prospect's problems or meet their needs. Use case studies or customer testimonials to demonstrate how your solution has helped others in similar situations.
5. Offer alternatives: If the prospect has a specific objection or concern, offer alternative solutions that address their needs or concerns. This can help to build trust and credibility, and may lead to a more constructive dialogue.
6. Maintain professionalism: No matter how the prospect responds, it's important to remain professional, respectful, and calm. Don't take objections personally or become defensive, and be willing to take a step back if the conversation becomes too heated or confrontational.

7 – How to Handle the Rejection as an IT Salesperson?

It is normal to face rejection as an IT salesperson, as not every sales pitch or interaction will result in a closed deal. Here are a few strategies for handling rejection in a healthy and productive way:

1. Acknowledge your emotions: It is natural to feel disappointed or frustrated when you are rejected, so it is important to take a moment to acknowledge and process these emotions.
2. Seek feedback: Ask the customer for specific reasons why they chose not to move forward with the sale, and use this feedback to identify areas for improvement in your sales approach.
3. Keep perspective: Remember that rejection is a normal part of the sales process, and try not to take it personally. Keep a positive attitude and stay focused on your goals.
4. Stay professional: Even if you are feeling upset or frustrated, make sure to remain professional and respectful in all your interactions with customers.

By following these strategies, you can help manage your emotions and keep your sales efforts on track even in the face of rejection.

8 – How to Handle the Pressure as an IT Salesperson?

Sales can be a high-pressure environment, and it is important to find healthy ways to manage stress and maintain a positive outlook. Here are a few strategies for handling pressure as an IT salesperson:

1. Set boundaries: Make sure to set aside time for rest and relaxation, and protect your work-life balance.

2. Stay organized: Having a clear plan and staying organized can help reduce stress and make it easier to manage your workload.
3. Find support: Build a network of colleagues, friends, or family members who you can turn to for support and encouragement.
4. Practice self-care: Make sure to prioritize your physical and mental well-being by eating well, getting enough sleep, and finding ways to relax and recharge.
5. Seek help if needed: If you are feeling overwhelmed or unable to cope with the demands of your job, don't hesitate to seek help from a mental health professional or other resources.

By following these strategies, you can help manage the pressure of being an IT salesperson and maintain a healthy and positive outlook.

9 – How to Handle the Success as an IT Salesperson?

Success in sales can be a rewarding and fulfilling experience, but it is important to handle it in a healthy and sustainable way. Here are a few strategies for managing success as an IT salesperson:

1. Celebrate your achievements: Take time to reflect on and celebrate your accomplishments, and share your success with others.

2. Keep a growth mindset: Don't rest on your laurels, and continue to learn and grow in your career.
3. Stay humble: Remember that success is often the result of teamwork and support from others, and be grateful for the help and opportunities you have received.
4. Stay focused: Don't let success go to your head, and continue to work hard and stay focused on your goals.
5. Give back: Consider using your success as an opportunity to help others, whether through mentorship, charitable work, or other forms of service.

By following these strategies, you can help ensure that your success as an IT salesperson is both rewarding and sustainable.

10 – How to Handle the Sales Manager as an IT Salesperson?

As an IT salesperson, it is important to maintain a positive and productive relationship with your sales manager. Here are a few strategies for handling your sales manager effectively:

1. Communicate openly: Keep your manager informed about your progress, any challenges you are facing, and any support you may need.
2. Seek feedback: Ask for feedback on your performance and be open to constructive criticism.
3. Set goals: Work with your manager to set clear measurable goals and objectives, and keep them

updated on your progress towards meeting those goals.
4. Be proactive: Take initiative and be proactive in identifying and pursuing sales opportunities.
5. Be a team player: Collaborate with your manager and other members of the sales team to contribute to the overall success of the group.

By following these strategies, you can help build a strong working relationship with your sales manager and achieve success in your role as an IT salesperson.

11 – How to Handle the C Level as an IT Salesperson?

C-level executives, such as CEOs, CFOs, and CTOs, are high-level decision makers within a company, and it can be challenging to gain their attention and secure their business as an IT salesperson. Here are a few strategies for handling C-level executives:

1. Do your research: Make sure you have a thorough understanding of the company and the specific needs and goals of the executive you are targeting.
2. Communicate clearly: Be concise and to-the-point in your communication, and be prepared to clearly articulate the value of your product or service.
3. Highlight the ROI: C-level executives are often concerned with the bottom line, so be prepared to explain how your product or service will generate a return on investment for the company.

4. Build rapport: Try to establish a personal connection with the executive, and look for common ground or shared interests.
5. Follow up: Be persistent but respectful in following up with the executive, and be prepared to address any objections they may have.

By following these strategies, you can effectively engage with C-level executives and increase your chances of securing their business.

12 – How to Handle the Customer Presentation as an IT Salesperson?

Customer presentations can be an important part of the sales process, as they provide an opportunity to showcase your products or services and persuade potential customers to make a purchase. Here are a few strategies for handling customer presentations effectively:

Prepare: Make sure you have a clear understanding of your products or services, and the needs and concerns of the customer. Practice your presentation to ensure that it is well-organized and polished.

1. Start strong: Begin your presentation with a strong opening that captures the attention of the audience and clearly states your purpose.
2. Use visual aids: Use slides, videos, or other visual aids to help illustrate your points and make your presentation more engaging.

3. Address objections: Be prepared to address any objections or concerns that the customer may have about your product or service.
4. End with a call to action: Make a clear and compelling case for why the customer should choose your product or service, and provide a clear next step for them to take.

By following these strategies, you can deliver a successful customer presentation and increase your chances of making a sale.

13 – How to Handle the Preparation of the Customer POC as an IT Salesperson?

A proof-of-concept (POC) is a demonstration of a product or service to a potential customer, designed to show how it meets their needs and solves their problems. Here are a few strategies for handling POCs effectively as an IT salesperson:

1. Research the customer: Make sure you have a thorough understanding of the customer's business, goals, and challenges, and how your product or service can help address them.
2. Understand the customer's needs: Make sure you have a thorough understanding of the customer's goals and challenges, and how your product or service can help address them.
3. Plan the demonstration: Outline the steps you will take to show the customer how your product or service works, and how it will solve their problems.

4. Gather materials: Collect any materials you will need for the demonstration, such as slides, videos, or product samples.
5. Test the product: Make sure the product or service is fully functional and ready for the demonstration.
6. Practice: Rehearse the demonstration to ensure that it is well-organized and flows smoothly.
7. Prepare a clear and concise demonstration: Plan out the steps you will take to show the customer how your product or service works, and be prepared to answer any questions they may have.
8. Highlight the success criteria and benefits: Make sure to clearly communicate the success criteria and benefits of your product or service to the customer, and how it compares to alternatives on the market.
9. Follow up after the POC: After the POC, follow up with the customer to see if they have any additional questions or concerns, and to discuss next steps.

By following these strategies, you can help ensure that the POC is a success and increase your chances of securing the customer's business.

14 – How to Handle the Foxes at the Customer Site as an IT Salesperson?

It is not uncommon for IT salespeople to encounter individuals or groups at a customer's site who may try to derail or interfere with the sales process. These individuals may be referred to as "foxes." Here are a few strategies for handling foxes effectively as an IT salesperson:

1. Identify the foxes: Pay attention to the dynamics at the customer site, and try to identify any individuals or groups who may be trying to obstruct the sales process.
2. Understand their motivations: Try to understand why the foxes are acting the way they are, and what they hope to gain by disrupting the process.
3. Focus on the customer: Keep the customer's needs and goals at the center of the conversation, and try to redirect the conversation back to how your product or service can help meet those needs.
4. Build allies: Seek out allies within the organization who can help support your sales efforts and counteract the influence of the foxes.
5. Stay professional: Even if the foxes are being difficult or confrontational, try to remain calm and professional, and avoid getting drawn into any personal conflicts.

By following these strategies, you can help navigate the challenges posed by foxes and stay focused on your sales goals.

15 – How to Find Out the Foxes at the Customer Site as an IT Salesperson?

To identify "foxes" at a customer's site, pay attention to the dynamics of the group and look for individuals or groups who may be trying to obstruct the sales process. Here are a few specific signs to look for:

1. They try to disrupt the conversation: Foxes may try to change the subject or introduce unrelated issues in an attempt to derail the sales process.
2. They are resistant to change: Foxes may be resistant to new ideas or solutions, and may try to block the adoption of your product or service.
3. They are difficult to please: Foxes may be overly critical or demanding, and may seem impossible to satisfy.
4. They are resistant to your presence: Foxes may try to exclude you from meetings or conversations, or may make it difficult for you to access the resources you need to do your job.

By paying attention to these behaviors, you can help identify foxes at the customer site and develop strategies for handling them effectively.

16 – How to Earn the Trust of the Foxes at the Customer Site as an IT Salesperson?

Earning the trust of "foxes" at a customer's site can be challenging, but it is important to try to build a positive and productive relationship with them. Here are a few strategies you can use to earn the trust of foxes:

1. Demonstrate your expertise: Show the foxes that you have a thorough understanding of your products or services and how they can solve the customer's problems.

2. Be transparent: Be open and honest with the foxes about your intentions and what you are offering, and be willing to address any concerns or objections they may have.
3. Show your value: Make it clear to the foxes how your product or service will benefit the customer, and how it compares to alternatives on the market.
4. Be responsive: Make an effort to address the foxes' needs and concerns in a timely and professional manner, and follow up as needed.
5. Build rapport: Try to find common ground or shared interests with the foxes, and work to establish a personal connection.

By following these strategies, you can help build trust and establish a productive relationship with the foxes at the customer site.

17 – What Are the Personal and the Organizational Agenda of the Foxes?

The personal agenda of "foxes" at a customer's site refers to the individual goals and motivations of those individuals. These may be related to career advancement, personal recognition, or other personal objectives.

The organizational agenda refers to the goals and priorities of the company as a whole. These may include increasing profits, expanding into new markets, or improving efficiency.

It is important for IT salespeople to try to understand both the personal and organizational agendas of foxes at a customer's site, as this can help inform strategies for dealing with them effectively and achieving success in the sales process.

18 – How to Find Out the Personal Agenda of the Foxes at the Customer Site as an IT Salesperson?

It can be helpful to try to understand the personal agenda of "foxes" at a customer's site, as this can help you anticipate their actions and develop strategies for dealing with them effectively. Here are a few ways you can try to uncover the personal agenda of foxes:

1. Ask questions: Try to ask open-ended questions and listen carefully to their responses to get a sense of their motivations and priorities.
2. Observe their behavior: Pay attention to how the foxes behave and interact with others, as this can give you clues about their personal agenda.
3. Seek feedback: Ask for feedback from other members of the sales team or the customer's organization to get a more well-rounded view of the foxes' motivations and behaviors.
4. Look for patterns: Try to identify any recurring themes or patterns in the foxes' actions or behaviors, as these may point to their underlying agenda.

By following these strategies, you can gain a better understanding of the personal agenda of the foxes at the customer site.

19 – How to Find Out the Organization Agenda of the Foxes?

To understand the organization agenda of "foxes" at a customer's site, you can try the following strategies:

1. Research the company: Gain a thorough understanding of the company's goals, priorities, and business model, and how the foxes fit into this structure.
2. Ask questions: Try to ask open-ended questions and listen carefully to their responses to get a sense of their role within the organization and what they are trying to achieve.
3. Observe their behavior: Pay attention to how the foxes behave and interact with others, and look for clues about their priorities and goals.
4. Seek feedback: Ask for feedback from other members of the sales team or the customer's organization to get a more well-rounded view of the foxes' motivations and behaviors.
5. Look for patterns: Try to identify any recurring themes or patterns in the foxes' actions or behaviors, as these may point to the organization's underlying agenda.

By following these strategies, you can gain a better understanding of the organization agenda of the foxes at the customer site.

20 – How to Convert a Fox to Coach?

While it's not always necessary or appropriate to convert a customer into a friend in the IT domain, building a friendly and positive relationship with them can help improve communication, trust, and satisfaction. Here are some tips for how to develop a friendly relationship with a customer in the IT domain:

1. Be approachable and friendly. Create a positive first impression by greeting the customer warmly, smiling, and showing genuine interest in their needs and concerns.
2. Establish rapport and build trust by being authentic, transparent, and honest in your interactions with the foxes.
3. Demonstrate your expertise and knowledge of the IT industry, and be willing to share insights and resources with the foxes.
4. Listen actively and empathetically. Take the time to really understand the customer's perspective, and respond with empathy and understanding.
5. Show the foxes how your products or services can solve their specific challenges and meet their needs.
6. Offer ongoing support and resources to the foxes to help them succeed with your products or services.
7. Communicate clearly and transparently. Keep the customer informed of progress, setbacks, and other relevant information, and avoid using technical jargon that they may not understand.

8. Be respectful and professional. Even if you become friendly with a customer, it's important to maintain a professional demeanor and respect their boundaries.
9. Look for common ground. Try to find shared interests or experiences that you can bond over, such as a favorite TV show, hobby, or travel destination.
10. Follow up with the foxes after the sale to ensure that they are satisfied with their purchase and to address any issues that may arise.
11. Show appreciation and gratitude. Express your thanks for the customer's business and loyalty, and let them know how much you value their support.

By building strong relationships with the foxes and demonstrating the value of your products or services, you can convert them into coaches who will support and advocate for your company.

21 – What Is a Sales Pitch?

A sales pitch is a persuasive message or presentation aimed at convincing a potential customer to buy a product or service. It typically highlights the benefits and features of the product or service and addresses the customer's needs and concerns in order to close a sale.

There are several types of sales pitch in the IT domain, including:

1. Product pitch: focuses on the features and benefits of a particular product or service.

2. Solution pitch: presents a solution to a specific problem or challenge the prospect is facing.
3. Consultative pitch: involves asking questions to understand the prospect's needs and then tailoring the pitch to those needs.
4. Competitive pitch: emphasizes the advantages of a particular product or service over those of its competitors.
5. ROI pitch: emphasizes the potential return on investment that the prospect could expect by purchasing the product or service.
6. Elevator pitch: a brief, compelling summary of a product or service that can be delivered in the time it takes to ride an elevator.

22 – What Is the Best Sales Pitch in IT Domain?

There is no one-size-fits-all "best" sales pitch in the IT domain, as the most effective pitch will depend on the specific product or service being sold, the needs and priorities of the prospective customer, and other factors. However, some effective strategies that can be used in IT sales pitches include:

1. Focusing on the benefits and outcomes of the product or service, rather than just the features.
2. Demonstrating how the product or service can address specific pain points or challenges that the prospective customer is facing.

3. Tailoring the pitch to the prospect's industry, role, and specific needs.
4. Using customer testimonials and case studies to demonstrate the value and success of the product or service.
5. Emphasizing the long-term value and return on investment that the product or service can provide.
6. Building rapport and establishing a personal connection with the prospect.
7. Highlighting any unique or innovative features of the product or service.

Ultimately, the most effective sales pitch will depend on the specific context and audience, and a successful IT salesman will be able to tailor their approach to meet the needs of each individual customer.

23 – How to Ask an Open-Ended Question to the Foxes at the Customer Site?

There are a few strategies you can use to ask open-ended questions to the foxes at the customer site as an IT salesperson:

1. Start with a broad, general question that allows the foxes to share their thoughts and experiences: "What challenges are you currently facing in your IT department?"
2. Use follow-up questions to dive deeper into specific areas of interest: "Can you tell me more about how you are currently handling [specific challenge]? What has been working well and what could be improved?"

3. Encourage the foxes to share their vision and goals: "What do you see as the future of IT at your organization? What goals do you have in mind for the next year or two?"
4. Use probing questions to get the foxes to think more deeply about their needs and challenges: "How have you addressed similar challenges in the past? What considerations do you take into account when making technology decisions?"

By using open-ended questions, you can encourage the foxes to share their thoughts and ideas, and gain a better understanding of their needs and challenges. This will help you tailor your sales pitch to better meet their needs and increase the likelihood of a successful sale.

24 – How to Use Positive Body Language as an IT Salesperson?

As an IT salesperson, you can use positive body language to build rapport with potential clients and convey confidence in your products and services. Here are a few tips for using positive body language as an IT salesperson:

1. Make eye contact: Maintaining eye contact shows that you are engaged in the conversation and helps build trust.
2. Use open body language: Stand or sit with an open posture, with your arms uncrossed and your palms facing up. This conveys openness and honesty.

3. Smile: A genuine smile can help put clients at ease and make you appear more approachable.
4. Use hand gestures: Use hand gestures to emphasize your points and show enthusiasm.
5. Lean in slightly: Leaning in slightly shows that you are interested in what the client has to say.

By using positive body language, you can build trust with clients and convey confidence in your products and services.

25 – What Is the Leadership Skills?

Leadership skills refer to the abilities and attributes that enable individuals to lead, motivate, and guide a team or group of people towards a common goal or vision. Some common leadership skills include:

1. Communication: Leaders should be able to effectively communicate their ideas, goals, and expectations to their team members.
2. Decision-making: Leaders should be able to make informed and timely decisions that benefit the team and the organization.
3. Visionary thinking: Leaders should be able to think strategically and develop a clear vision for their team and organization.
4. Adaptability: Leaders should be able to adapt to changes in the environment and adjust their strategies accordingly.

5. Empathy: Leaders should be able to understand and empathize with their team members' needs and concerns.
6. Accountability: Leaders should take responsibility for their decisions and actions, and hold themselves and their team members accountable for their work.
7. Motivation: Leaders should be able to inspire and motivate their team members to achieve their best performance.
8. Delegation: Leaders should be able to delegate tasks and responsibilities effectively, while also providing guidance and support to their team members.
9. Conflict resolution: Leaders should be able to manage conflicts and resolve disputes among team members.
10. Continuous learning: Leaders should be committed to continuous learning and self-improvement to stay up-to-date with industry trends and best practices.

These skills are essential for effective leadership and can be developed and improved over time through training, coaching, and experience.

26 – What Are the Descriptions of an IT Businessman?

An IT businessman is an individual or professional who is involved in the ownership, management, or operation of a business that is related to information technology (IT). The specific responsibilities and duties of an IT businessman may vary depending on the type and size of the business, but some key characteristics include:

1. Business acumen: Understanding of business principles and financial management, in order to make strategic decisions that will drive the growth of the business.
2. IT knowledge: Knowledge of the IT industry and the products or services offered by the business.
3. Entrepreneurial spirit: A willingness to take risks and innovate in order to grow the business.
4. Leadership skills: Strong leadership skills and the ability to manage and motivate a team.
5. Strategic thinking: The ability to think strategically and make decisions that will have a positive impact on the business.
6. Sales and marketing: Understanding of sales and marketing techniques, to promote and grow the business.
7. Networking: Strong networking skills, to build relationships with potential customers and partners.
8. Adaptability: The ability to adapt to changing market conditions and stay ahead of the competition.
9. Technical Understanding: Understanding of the technical aspects of the business, such as software development, IT infrastructure, and security.
10. Business Development: Identifying and developing new business opportunities through partnerships, joint ventures, and other strategic relationships.

An IT businessman is responsible for leading the business, making strategic decisions and driving the growth of the company, by identifying new opportunities, creating new products or services and developing new markets. They also need to have a good understanding of the market trends, customers and competition.

27 – What Is Hunter Salesman and Farmer Salesman?

In the IT domain, the terms "Hunter Salesman" and "Farmer Salesman" are often used to describe different approaches to sales.

A Hunter Salesman is someone who is focused on acquiring new customers and closing deals. They are often more aggressive and proactive in their sales approach, seeking out potential leads and making cold calls to generate interest. Hunter salespeople are typically good at identifying new opportunities and closing deals quickly, but they may not have as strong of a relationship with their clients.

On the other hand, a Farmer Salesman is someone who is focused on nurturing existing relationships with customers to generate repeat business and build long-term loyalty. They are often more patient and relationship-driven in their sales approach, taking the time to understand their customers' needs and providing personalized solutions. Farmer salespeople are typically good at building strong, lasting relationships with clients, but they may not be as effective at generating new business.

Both approaches can be effective in the IT industry, depending on the company's goals and the type of products or services being sold. Some companies may prefer a Hunter Salesman approach if they are looking to quickly expand their customer base, while others may prefer a Farmer Salesman approach if they are looking to build strong, long-term relationships with their existing clients.

28 – How to Be Hunter Salesman?

To be a successful Hunter Salesman in the IT domain, you need to have a specific set of skills and qualities. Here are some tips that can help you become a Hunter Salesman:

1. Understand your target market: It is essential to understand the needs and challenges of your target market to identify potential opportunities for your product or service. Research and analyze your target audience's behavior and preferences to find the best approach to sell your products.
2. Develop a strong pitch: Your pitch needs to be clear, concise, and tailored to your potential customers' needs. Highlight the key benefits of your product or service and how it can help your clients solve their problems.
3. Build a robust network: Develop a robust network of potential clients and industry contacts. Attend industry events, meetups, and conferences to network and generate new leads. Build relationships with potential clients through personalized communications, such as emails, phone calls, or social media.
4. Be proactive: A Hunter Salesman is always on the lookout for new opportunities. Don't wait for clients to come to you; reach out to potential clients and be proactive in your approach.
5. Be persistent: A successful Hunter Salesman never gives up. If a potential client is not interested in your product or service, follow up with them and continue

to nurture the relationship. Persistence pays off in the long run.
6. Be knowledgeable: In the IT domain, it's essential to stay up-to-date with the latest trends, technologies, and industry news. Develop a deep understanding of your product or service and be able to articulate its value to your clients.

Overall, being a Hunter Salesman requires a combination of skills, including strong communication, persistence, industry knowledge, and the ability to build relationships. By mastering these skills, you can become a successful salesperson in the IT domain.

29 – How to Be a Farmer Salesman?

To be a successful Farmer Salesman in the IT domain, you need to focus on building strong relationships with your clients and providing personalized solutions that meet their needs. Here are some tips that can help you become a Farmer Salesman:

1. Develop a deep understanding of your clients: To build a long-term relationship with your clients, you need to understand their needs, preferences, and pain points. Spend time talking to your clients, asking them questions, and actively listening to their responses.
2. Build trust: Trust is a crucial element in any business relationship. Be honest and transparent with your clients, and always follow through on your

commitments. Focus on providing value to your clients, rather than just selling products.
3. Provide exceptional customer service: In the IT domain, customer service is critical. Be responsive to your clients' needs, answer their questions promptly, and provide personalized solutions that meet their specific requirements.
4. Communicate regularly: Stay in touch with your clients on a regular basis. Send them personalized communications, such as newsletters or updates on new products or services that may be of interest to them. Be available to answer their questions and address any concerns they may have.
5. Offer ongoing support: Once you have sold a product or service to a client, don't just move on to the next sale. Offer ongoing support to your clients, such as training, troubleshooting, or maintenance services.
6. Build a referral network: Word of mouth is a powerful marketing tool. Build a network of satisfied clients who can refer new business to you. Offer incentives, such as discounts or rewards, to clients who refer new customers to you.

Overall, being a successful Farmer Salesman in the IT domain requires a strong focus on building relationships, providing exceptional customer service, and offering ongoing support. By mastering these skills, you can become a trusted advisor to your clients and build long-lasting, profitable relationships.

Chapter 3

How to Handle the RIGHT Customer?

1 – How to Sharp the Ax Before Facing a Customer in IT Domain?

"Sharpening the ax before facing a customer" is a metaphor that refers to being prepared and well-informed before meeting with a customer. In the IT domain, some strategies for sharpening the ax before facing a customer include:

1. Researching the customer: Before meeting with a customer, research their company, industry, and specific needs. This will help you tailor your pitch and address their specific pain points.
2. Familiarizing yourself with the product or service: Be sure that you are fully familiar with the features, benefits and limitations of the product or service you will be discussing with the customer.
3. Anticipating objections and concerns: Think about potential objections or concerns the customer may have, and prepare responses in advance.

4. Reviewing the customer's history: Review any previous interactions or transactions you've had with the customer, and use this information to inform your approach.
5. Being up-to-date with the industry and technology: Stay current with the latest industry trends and technological developments in the IT domain, so that you can offer the most relevant and up-to-date solutions to the customer.
6. Preparing a detailed and well-structured proposal: Having a detailed and well-structured proposal that highlights the value of your product or service, can help you to make a strong and convincing pitch

By taking the time to prepare and sharpen the ax before facing a customer, you will be better equipped to address their specific needs and concerns, and to close the sale.

2 – How to Sharpen My Ax Every Morning?

Sharpening your ax every morning is a metaphor for taking the time each day to prepare and improve yourself, so that you are well-equipped to face the day's challenges. In the IT domain, some strategies for sharpening your ax every morning include:

1. Reviewing the previous day's work: Take time to review what you accomplished the day before, what went well, and what could have been done better. Use this information to inform your approach to the day ahead.

2. Staying informed: Make sure you are up-to-date with the latest industry trends and technological developments. This will help you stay current and relevant in your field.
3. Reflecting on your skills: Take time to reflect on your skills, and identify areas where you need to improve. This may include taking online courses, attending workshops or networking with colleagues.
4. Reviewing your goals: Review your goals for the day, week and month, and make a plan for how to achieve them.
5. Preparing for upcoming meetings or calls: Review any upcoming meetings or calls you have scheduled, and prepare any necessary materials or information.
6. Organizing your workspace: Make sure your workspace is clean, organized and conducive to productivity.

By taking the time each morning to sharpen your ax, you will be better equipped to face the day's challenges, and to achieve your goals. This will help you to maintain a competitive edge and be more successful in your IT career.

3 – How to Motivate Myself Every Morning?

Motivating yourself every morning can be a challenge, but it is important for achieving success in your career. Here are some strategies you can use to motivate yourself every morning:

1. Set clear and achievable goals: Identify specific, measurable and achievable goals for the day, week and month, and make a plan to achieve them. Having clear goals can give you a sense of purpose and direction.
2. Create a morning routine: Having a consistent morning routine can help you start your day on the right foot. This can include things like exercising, meditating, or journaling.
3. Positive affirmations: Repeat positive affirmations to yourself to build confidence and boost motivation.
4. Surround yourself with positivity: Surround yourself with positive people, images, and messages that inspire and uplift you.
5. Give yourself a reward: Set up a system of rewards for yourself for achieving your goals. This could be something as simple as a piece of candy or a favorite drink at the end of the day.
6. Reflect on your past achievements: Take time to reflect on your past achievements and remind yourself of how capable you are.
7. Listen to uplifting music or podcast: Listening to uplifting music or a podcast can help to boost your mood and motivation.
8. Get enough sleep: Getting enough sleep is essential for maintaining good physical and mental health, and can help you feel more energized and motivated in the morning.

By implementing these strategies, you can learn how to motivate yourself every morning and increase your chances of achieving your goals. Remember to be patient with yourself, and that it takes time to develop a routine that works for you.

4 – How to Plan Your Day as an IT Salesman?

Planning your day as an IT salesperson can involve several steps to make the most of your time and increase your chances of closing deals. Here are some tips for planning your day:

1. Prioritize your tasks: Start by identifying the most important tasks that need to be completed that day. Prioritize them based on their urgency and potential impact on your sales.
2. Set clear goals: Set specific, measurable, and achievable goals for the day. These could include making a certain number of calls, setting up a specific number of meetings, or closing a certain number of deals.
3. Use a CRM: Utilize a customer relationship management (CRM) system to manage your contacts, track your progress, and prioritize your tasks.
4. Schedule time for prospecting: Set aside time each day to research and identify new potential customers.
5. Make use of technology: Use email, social media, and other digital tools to communicate with potential customers and make the sales process more efficient

6. Schedule follow-up tasks: Set reminders for follow-up tasks, such as sending follow-up emails or making follow-up calls to leads.
7. Schedule time for training and development: Set aside time for ongoing training and professional development to stay current on industry trends and improve your sales skills.
8. Review progress and adjust: At the end of the day, review your progress and adjust your plan as needed for the next day.

By following these tips, you can create a daily plan that maximizes your time and helps you hit your sales goals.

5 – Engorging Statements for IT Salesmen.

Engaging statements, can be used by IT salespeople to capture the attention of potential customers and persuade them to take action, such as purchasing a product or service. Here are a few examples of engaging statements that an IT salesperson might use:

1. "Our software solutions will help your business increase efficiency and reduce costs."
2. "Our software solutions will help your organization achieve its digital transformation goals."
3. "Our cybersecurity services will protect your company from cyber threats and keep your data safe."
4. "With our cybersecurity services, you can rest easy knowing your sensitive data is protected."

5. "Our consulting services can help your organization take advantage of the latest technology trends to stay competitive."
6. "Our consulting services can help your company stay ahead of the competition with the latest technology."
7. "Our cloud-based solutions will give your business the flexibility and scalability it needs to grow."
8. "Our cloud-based services will provide your organization with the flexibility and scalability it needs to grow."
9. "Our IT support services will keep your company's technology running smoothly, so you can focus on what really matters."
10. "Our IT support team is always ready to assist you, so you can focus on your core business."
11. "Our AI-powered software will help your company boost productivity and gain insights"
12. "Our IT project management services ensure that your company's technology initiatives are delivered on-time, on-budget, and to your satisfaction."
13. "Our IT project management team ensures that your technology initiatives are delivered on-time and within budget."
14. "Our platform offers AI-based solutions that will help your organization improve operational efficiency and gain insights for better decision making"

Engaging statements, also known as value propositions, can be used to capture the attention of IT customers and persuade them to take action, such as purchasing a product or service. Here are a few examples of engaging statements that an IT company might use to target their customers:

6 – How to Treat an Existing Customer?

It is important to prioritize and provide excellent service to existing customers, as they can be a valuable source of repeat business and positive word-of-mouth marketing. Here are a few strategies you can use to treat existing customers well:

1. Respond to their inquiries and requests promptly and professionally.
2. Offer personalized service and go the extra mile to meet their needs.
3. Keep them informed about new products or services that may be of interest to them.
4. Show appreciation for their business and value them as a customer.
5. Solve any problems or issues they may have in a timely and satisfactory manner.

By following these strategies, you can help build long-term relationships with your customers and keep them happy and loyal.

7 – How to Treat a New Customer?

Here are a few strategies you can use to treat new customers well:

1. Make a good first impression: Greet the customer warmly, be friendly and professional, and make sure to listen to their needs and concerns.
2. Provide clear and helpful information: Answer the customer's questions fully and accurately, and provide any additional resources or information they may need.
3. Offer personalized recommendations: Suggest products or services that may be of particular interest to the customer based on their needs and preferences.
4. Follow up after the sale: Check in with the customer to see if they have any additional questions or concerns, and make sure they are satisfied with their purchase.

By following these strategies, you can help build trust and establish long-term relationships with your new customers.

8 – How to Be a Positive Thinker?

Being a positive thinker can have many benefits, including improved mental and physical health, better relationships, and increased success in your personal and professional life. Here are some strategies for developing a positive mindset:

1. Practice gratitude: Make a habit of regularly reflecting on the things you are thankful for. This can help shift your focus from negative to positive.
2. Reframe negative thoughts: When negative thoughts arise, try to reframe them in a positive light. For

example, instead of thinking, "I can't do this," try thinking, "I can do this, and I will figure out a way."
3. Surround yourself with positivity: Spend time with positive people, read inspiring books, and engage with uplifting content on social media.
4. Practice mindfulness: Mindfulness techniques such as meditation and deep breathing can help you become more present and aware, and reduce stress and negative emotions.
5. Take care of yourself: Make sure you are getting enough sleep, eating well, and engaging in regular physical activity. Taking care of your physical health can have a positive impact on your mental well-being.
6. Find humor in difficult situations: Try to find something to laugh about, even in difficult situations. This can help to lighten the mood and put things in perspective.
7. Help others: Helping others can be a powerful way to boost your own mood and feelings of positivity.
8. Keep a positive attitude: Stay optimistic and maintain a positive attitude, even when things don't go as planned. Remember that every setback is an opportunity to learn and grow.

It is important to note that it takes time and practice to develop a positive mindset, and it's not always easy. Be kind and patient with yourself, and remember that setbacks are a natural part of the process. Keep working on it and you'll find that you'll be able to have a more positive outlook on life.

9 – What Are the Main Values to have an Emotional Intelligent Behavior?

Emotional intelligence (EI) is the ability to recognize, understand, and manage one's own emotions, as well as the emotions of others. Having emotional intelligence can help individuals navigate through personal and professional relationships, communicate more effectively, and make better decisions. The main values of having an emotionally intelligent behavior include:

1. Self-awareness: Being aware of one's own emotions, thoughts, and behaviors, and understanding how they affect others.
2. Self-regulation: Being able to control one's own emotions and reactions, and being able to manage stress in a healthy way.
3. Empathy: Being able to understand and relate to the emotions of others, and being able to put oneself in their shoes.
4. Social Skills: Being able to communicate effectively, build and maintain relationships, and collaborate with others.
5. Motivation: Being able to use emotions to drive action, set and achieve goals, and maintain a positive outlook.
6. Adaptability: being able to adapt to changing circumstances, being open to new perspectives and willing to learn from experience.

Having emotional intelligence can help individuals to be more successful in personal and professional relationships, to be more effective communicator, to be a better leader and to make better decisions. it also helps in problem solving, stress management, and conflict resolution. Emotional intelligence is also considered as key for personal growth and development, and for achieving overall well-being.

10 – How to Learn Emotional Intelligent Behavior?

Learning emotional intelligence (EI) is a process that involves developing the ability to recognize, understand, and manage one's own emotions and the emotions of others. Here are some ways to learn EI:

1. Reflect on your own emotions: Take time to reflect on how you feel and how your emotions affect your thoughts and actions. This will help you to become more self-aware.
2. Practice self-regulation: Develop techniques to manage your emotions, such as deep breathing, meditation, or exercise. This will help you to control your reactions and manage stress in a healthy way.
3. Learn to empathize: Practice putting yourself in other people's shoes, and try to understand their emotions and perspectives. This will help you to develop empathy.
4. Improve your communication skills: Practice active listening, expressing yourself clearly, and giving and receiving feedback. This will help you to communicate more effectively.

5. Develop your social skills: Practice building and maintaining relationships, collaborating with others, and leading teams. This will help you to build a strong network of relationships.
6. Learn from failure: Embrace failure as a learning opportunity, and try to identify the emotions that led to it. This will help you to adapt to new situations and to be more open to new perspectives.
7. Read and Learn: Reading books and articles on emotional intelligence, attending workshops and seminars on the topic, or seeking guidance from a therapist or coach can also help in learning EI.

Remember that learning EI is an ongoing process and it requires consistent effort and practice. It's important to keep in mind that learning emotional intelligence is not a one-time event, it's a life-long journey.

11 – What to Do to Have an Emotional Intelligent Behavior?

To develop and maintain an emotionally intelligent behavior, you can follow these steps:

1. Practice self-awareness: Take time to reflect on your own emotions, thoughts, and behaviors, and understand how they affect others.
2. Self-regulation: Learn to manage your emotions and reactions, practice techniques like deep breathing, meditation or exercise to control your emotions.

3. Empathy: Practice putting yourself in other people's shoes, try to understand their emotions and perspectives.
4. Improve communication: Develop effective communication skills, practice active listening, and give and receive feedback.
5. Build relationships: Work on building and maintaining relationships, collaborate with others, and lead teams.
6. Be adaptable: Be open to new perspectives, be willing to learn from failure and be adaptable to changing circumstances.
7. Learn from others: Seek guidance and feedback from people you trust and respect, learn from their experiences and try to apply what you learn to your own behavior.
8. Seek professional help: if you find it difficult to develop EI, consider seeking the help of a therapist or coach who can guide you through the process.

Remember that developing emotional intelligence is a journey that takes time, effort and practice. It's important to be patient with yourself and to give yourself credit for the progress you make. Emotional intelligence is a set of skills that can be developed, enhanced and improved over time.

12 – How to Sell Value to Your Customer?

Selling value in the IT domain involves highlighting the benefits and advantages of a product or service and showing how it can help the customer achieve their goals and solve their pain points. Some strategies for selling value in the IT domain include:

1. Understanding the customer's specific needs and pain points: By gathering information through open-ended questions, you can understand the customer's specific challenges and tailor your pitch to address those needs.
2. Positioning your product or service as a solution: Show the customer how your product or service can help them solve their pain points and achieve their goals. Provide real-world examples and case studies to illustrate the value of your solution.
3. Highlighting the ROI: Show the customer the potential return on investment (ROI) they can expect from using your product or service. Provide them with concrete numbers and data to demonstrate the value of your solution.
4. Differentiating yourself from the competition: Show the customer how your product or service is unique and provides more value than similar solutions offered by your competitors.
5. Building a long-term relationship: Building a long-term relationship with the customer demonstrates that you are invested in their success and will be there to support them after the sale. It also opens the door for upselling and cross-selling opportunities in the future.
6. Staying up to date with industry trends and changes Keeping up with the latest technology and industry developments will ensure that you can offer the most current and relevant solutions to your customers.

By highlighting the value of your IT products and services, you can help the customer see the potential benefits they can gain by using them and, in turn, increase the chances of closing the sale.

13 – How to Perfect Your IT Sales Pitch Introduction with Your Customer?

1. Start with a strong opening: Begin with a statement that grabs the listener's attention and makes them want to hear more.
2. Identify the problem: Clearly and succinctly explain the problem or need that your product or service addresses.
3. Position your solution: Highlight how your product or service addresses the problem and how it is unique and better than other options.
4. Use customer testimonials: Including customer testimonials can help to build credibility and demonstrate the value of your product or service.
5. Use simple and easy-to-understand language: Avoid using jargon or technical terms that the listener may not understand.
6. Keep it short and to the point: A good sales pitch should be short and to the point, focusing on the most important information.
7. Ask questions: Asking questions can help to keep the listener engaged and can also provide valuable information that can be used to tailor the pitch to the listener's needs.

8. Show enthusiasm: Show your enthusiasm and belief in your product or service, it will help the listener to be more interested in it.
9. Provide a call to action: End the pitch with a clear call to action, such as scheduling a follow-up meeting or request for a proposal.
10. Practice: Practice delivering your pitch multiple times, and gather feedback from others to improve it.

It's important to remember that a good sales pitch is tailored to the listener and their specific needs, and that it's not about hard selling but about solving the customer's problem.

14 – How to Make a Successful Sales Call in IT Domain?

Making a successful sales call in the IT domain requires a combination of effective preparation, communication, and relationship-building strategies. Here are a few steps you can take to make a successful sales call:

1. Prepare for the call: Research the customer's company and industry, as well as their specific needs and pain points, this will help you tailor your sales pitch and address their concerns.
2. Build rapport: Start the call with small talk and establish a connection with the customer to build trust and make them more receptive to your message.
3. Communicate your value proposition: Clearly communicate the value your IT products or services

can bring to the customer, and explain how they can address their specific needs and pain points.
4. Listen actively: Listen actively to the customer and understand their needs, this is crucial for addressing their concerns and objections.
5. Address objections: Anticipate and address any objections or concerns the customer may have, this can help overcome roadblocks to the sale.
6. Close the sale: Use effective closing techniques, such as the "Assumptive Close" or "Reason Why Close," to close the sale.
7. Follow up: Follow up with the customer after the call to answer any remaining questions and solidify the sale.
8. Personalize the call: Tailor the sales pitch to the customer's specific needs and pain points, and use your product knowledge to demonstrate the benefits of your IT products or services.
9. Use a consultative approach: Approach the call as a consultation, ask questions and understand the customer's needs and tailor your pitch accordingly.
10. Provide relevant and useful information: Provide relevant and useful information to the customer, this will help establish credibility, build trust and increase the likelihood of closing a deal.

15 – What Are the Tips for Making a Successful Sales Call in IT Domain?

Here are a few tips for making a successful sales call in the IT domain:

1. Know your audience: Understand the customer's company, industry and specific needs and pain points.
2. Be prepared: Have all the necessary information about your IT products or services and be able to demonstrate the value they can bring to the customer.
3. Build a connection: Start the call with small talk and establish a connection with the customer to build trust and make them more receptive to your message.
4. Listen actively: Listen actively to the customer and understand their needs, this is crucial for addressing their concerns and objections.
5. Be solutions oriented: Offer solutions that address the customer's specific needs and pain points.
6. Be prepared to handle objections: Anticipate and be prepared to address any objections or concerns the customer may have.
7. Use effective closing techniques: Use effective closing techniques, such as the "Assumptive Close" or "Reason Why Close," to close the sale.
8. Follow-up: Follow-up with the customer after the call to answer any remaining questions and solidify the sale.
9. Use a consultative approach: Approach the call as a consultation, ask questions and understand the customer's needs and tailor your pitch accordingly.
10. Build relationships: Build a relationship with the customer and establish trust to increase the likelihood of future sales opportunities.
11. Use technology: Use technology such as customer relationship management systems, to track customer

interactions and sales activities, and automate repetitive tasks and processes.
12. Continuously improve: Continuously improve and adapt your sales approach by testing new methods, measuring results and making adjustments accordingly.

16 – What Are the Descriptions of an IT Customer?

An IT customer is an individual or organization that purchases products or services related to information technology (IT). The specific characteristics of an IT customer may vary depending on the type of business or organization, but some key descriptions include:

1. Technological needs: They have specific IT needs that must be met, such as software, hardware, or IT services.
2. Budget constraints: They operate within a budget and need to ensure that the products or services they purchase provide value for the cost.
3. Technical understanding: They have a basic understanding of technology and the products or services they are purchasing.
4. Security concerns: They are concerned about the security of their data and the products or services they are purchasing should be able to meet their security requirements.

5. Support needs: They need support with the products or services they purchase, including installation, training, and ongoing maintenance.
6. Technical evaluation: They evaluate products or services based on their technical features and benefits.
7. Innovation: They are interested in new and innovative products or services that can help them improve their operations and stay competitive.
8. Vendor evaluation: They evaluate vendors based on factors such as reputation, customer service, and industry experience.
9. Scalability: They require solutions that can scale to meet their changing business needs.
10. Compliance: They have compliance requirements that the products or services they purchase.

17 – Customer Relationship Management (CRM) System

A Customer Relationship Management (CRM) system is designed to help businesses manage interactions with customers and prospects. The main functions of a CRM system include:

1. Contact management: storing and organizing information about customers and prospects, such as contact information, communication history, and buying history.

2. Sales management: tracking sales opportunities, forecasting revenue, and analyzing sales performance.
3. Marketing automation: creating and executing marketing campaigns, tracking the effectiveness of marketing efforts, and measuring return on investment.
4. Service and support: managing customer service requests, tracking and resolving customer issues, and managing knowledge base.
5. Analytics and reporting: generating reports and dashboards to provide insights into customer behavior, sales performance, and marketing effectiveness.
6. Collaboration: allows team members to share data and communicate with each other to improve teamwork and coordination.
7. Mobile and Social CRM: CRM software can be accessed on mobile devices and also integrates with social media platforms to track customer interactions and engagement.

18 – Consultative Selling

Consultative selling is a customer-focused approach that involves actively listening to the customer's needs and concerns, and then offering solutions that meet those needs. Some common strategies used in consultative selling include: Identifying and understanding the customer's pain points and goals.

1. Building trust and rapport with the customer.
2. Asking open-ended questions to gather information and uncover the customer's needs.
3. Presenting solutions that align with the customer's needs and goals.
4. Addressing objections and concerns in a way that highlights the value of your solution.
5. Continuously following up and checking in with the customer to ensure they are satisfied with your solution and to identify any additional needs.

Note that consultative selling is a process and it's not only about closing the sale but also about building a long-term relationship with the customer.

19 – What Are the Open-Ended Questions in IT Domain?

Open-ended questions are questions that cannot be answered with a simple "yes" or "no" and require the person being asked to provide a more detailed or elaborate response. In the IT domain, some examples of open-ended questions that a salesperson might ask include:

1. Can you tell me about your current IT infrastructure and any pain points you're experiencing?
2. How do you currently handle [specific IT challenge or process], and what are the biggest challenges you face?
3. Can you walk me through your IT budgeting and decision-making process?

4. How do you measure the success of your IT initiatives and what metrics do you use?
5. Can you describe your company's IT goals for the next few years and how do you plan to achieve them?
6. Can you tell me about any upcoming IT projects or initiatives you're currently working on?

These are just a few examples and depending on the specific IT product or service being sold, the salesperson may need to ask more specific or targeted questions. The goal is to understand the customer's unique needs and pain points, and tailor the sales pitch to address those needs.

20 – How to Sell Value in IT Domain?

Selling value in the IT domain involves highlighting the benefits and advantages of a product or service and showing how it can help the customer achieve their goals and solve their pain points. Some strategies for selling value in the IT domain include:

1. Understanding the customer's specific needs and pain points: By gathering information through open-ended questions, you can understand the customer's specific challenges and tailor your pitch to address those needs.
2. Positioning your product or service as a solution: Show the customer how your product or service can help them solve their pain points and achieve their goals. Provide real-world examples and case studies to illustrate the value of your solution.

3. Highlighting the ROI: Show the customer the potential return on investment (ROI) they can expect from using your product or service. Provide them with concrete numbers and data to demonstrate the value of your solution.
4. Differentiating yourself from the competition: Show the customer how your product or service is unique and provides more value than similar solutions offered by your competitors.
5. Building a long-term relationship: Building a long-term relationship with the customer demonstrates that you are invested in their success and will be there to support them after the sale. It also opens the door for upselling and cross-selling opportunities in the future.
6. Staying up to date with industry trends and changes: Keeping up with the latest technology and industry developments will ensure that you can offer the most current and relevant solutions to your customers.

By highlighting the value of your IT products and services, you can help the customer see the potential benefits they can gain by using them and, in turn, increase the chances of closing the sale.

21 – How to Present Your Solution to Your Customer?

Presenting an IT solution to a customer is an important part of the sales process, as it enables sales professionals to demonstrate the value and benefits of the solution to potential customers. Here are some tips for presenting an IT solution to a customer:

1. Understand the customer's needs: Before presenting the solution, take the time to fully understand the customer's needs and challenges. This will help you tailor your presentation to their specific needs and show how the solution can meet those needs.
2. Use clear, concise language: Avoid using jargon or overly technical language, and focus on using clear and concise language that is easy for the customer to understand.
3. Use visuals: Use visuals such as slides, diagrams, or demos to help illustrate your points and make the presentation more engaging.
4. Emphasize the benefits: Focus on the benefits of the solution rather than the features, and be sure to highlight how it can solve the customer's specific needs and challenges.
5. Answer questions: Encourage the customer to ask questions, and be prepared to answer any questions they may have about the solution.

Overall, the key to presenting an IT solution to a customer is to understand their needs, use clear and concise language, and emphasize the benefits of the solution. By following these tips, sales professionals can effectively present IT solutions to customers and persuade them to make a purchase.

22 – How to Keep the Deal Moving with Your Customer?

Keeping a deal moving in the IT domain can be achieved by following these steps:

1. Communicate regularly: Establish regular communication with the customer to ensure that all parties are on the same page and that any issues or concerns are addressed in a timely manner.
2. Set clear milestones: Set clear milestones for the project and ensure that all parties are aware of their responsibilities and timelines. This will help to keep the project on track and on schedule.
3. Provide regular updates: Provide regular updates to the customer on the progress of the project, and address any issues or concerns that may arise.
4. Resolve issues promptly: Address and resolve any issues or problems that may arise during the project in a timely manner.
5. Deliver on time: Ensure that the project is delivered on time and to the customer's satisfaction.
6. Follow up after delivery: Follow up with the customer after delivery to ensure that they are satisfied with the product or service and to address any post-delivery issues or concerns.
7. Maintain a good relationship: Maintain a good relationship with the customer and continue to provide excellent service and support.
8. Look for upselling opportunities: Look for opportunities to upsell or cross-sell additional products or services to the customer.

By following these steps, you can keep the deal moving and increase the chances of closing the deal in the IT domain. Additionally, a good project management and a clear project plan with all stakeholders involved,

23 – Who Is the Right Customer to an IT Salesman?

The "right" customer for an IT salesman is a customer who:

1. Has a need for the IT products or services being offered: This means that the customer has a problem or challenge that the IT salesman's products or services can help solve.
2. Has the budget and decision-making power to purchase: The customer should have the financial resources and authority to make a purchase.
3. Is a good fit for the IT salesman's business: The customer's needs and business goals should align with the IT salesman's capabilities and areas of expertise.
4. Is open to communication and collaboration: The customer should be willing to engage in a dialogue with the IT salesman, and be open to working together to find solutions.
5. Is willing to take a risk: Some customers may be hesitant to try new technologies or solutions, but the right customer is willing to take a risk on something that has the potential to bring significant benefits.

6. Is open to ongoing support and partnership: The right customer is interested in building a long-term relationship with the IT salesman, rather than just making a one-time purchase.
7. What is a Key Account in IT Business?
8. In the IT industry, a key account is a customer that is particularly important to a business. Key accounts are often large, long-term customers that generate a significant portion of the company's revenue. They may also be strategic partners who play a vital role in the company's overall business operations.
9. Key accounts are typically managed differently than other accounts, as they require a higher level of attention and resources. The IT business may assign dedicated account managers or teams to handle key accounts, and may also develop special pricing or support packages to retain their business.
10. Managing key accounts effectively can be critical to the success of an IT business, as they can provide a stable source of revenue and help the business grow. On the other hand, losing a key account can have a significant negative impact on the company's financial performance.

24 – How to Evaluate the Customer in IT Domain?

Evaluating customers in IT sales domain is an important step in the sales process. It helps sales professionals to understand the customer's needs, goals, and pain points, and tailor their sales pitch accordingly. Here are some effective ways to evaluate customers in IT sales domain:

1. Conduct research: Before engaging with a customer, conduct research on their company, industry, and competitors. Use this information to understand their business goals and challenges, and identify how your product or service can provide value.
2. Ask questions: Ask open-ended questions that encourage the customer to share their needs, goals, and pain points. Listen actively to their responses and ask follow-up questions to gain a deeper understanding of their situation.
3. Analyze behavior: Analyze the customer's behavior, such as their communication style, decision-making process, and level of engagement. Use this information to tailor your approach and communication style to their preferences.
4. Review previous interactions: Review any previous interactions the customer has had with your company, such as emails, phone calls, or demos. Use this information to understand their level of interest and engagement, and tailor your sales pitch accordingly.
5. Evaluate budget: Evaluate the customer's budget and purchasing authority to understand their level of investment and decision-making power. This information will help you to determine the appropriate pricing and negotiation strategy.
6. Assess fit: Assess the fit between your product or service and the customer's needs, goals, and pain points. Determine whether your solution is a good

match for their specific situation, and address any potential concerns or objections they may have.

Overall, evaluating customers in IT sales domain requires a strategic and consultative approach that focuses on understanding their needs, goals, and pain points. By effectively evaluating customers, you can tailor your sales pitch to their specific situation, build trust and credibility, and ultimately close more deals.

25 – How to Build a Relationship with Your Customer?

Building a relationship with an IT prospect can be a great way to establish trust and credibility, which can help you close deals and build a successful business. Here are a few tips for building a relationship with an IT prospect:

1. Communicate regularly: Make sure to keep in touch with your prospect through email, phone calls, and in-person meetings. This will help you stay top of mind and build rapport.
2. Offer value: Look for ways to add value to your prospect's business by providing them with valuable information, resources, or insights. This could include sharing industry news, offering product demos, or providing expert advice.
3. Be responsive: When a prospect reaches out to you, make sure to respond promptly and professionally. This shows that you value their business and are dedicated to helping them succeed.

4. Build trust: Trust is an important factor in any business relationship, especially in the IT industry. Be transparent, honest, and reliable in all your interactions with your prospect.
5. Get to know them: Take the time to learn about your prospect's business and their needs. This will help you tailor your approach and offer solutions that are relevant and valuable to them.

26 – How to Build a Long-Term Relationship with Customer in IT Domain?

Building a long-term relationship with customers in the IT domain involves creating a positive and lasting impression, providing excellent customer service, and continuously delivering value. Some strategies for building a long-term relationship with IT customers include:

1. Providing exceptional customer service: Respond to customer inquiries and concerns promptly and professionally, and be available to address any issues that may arise.
2. Continuously delivering value: Continuously check-in with the customer and find ways to provide additional value such as through training, maintenance, and technical support.
3. Building trust: Be transparent and honest in all your interactions with the customer, and follow through on any commitments you make.
4. Being a trusted advisor: Act as a trusted advisor to the customer by staying up-to-date on industry trends and

changes, and by providing valuable insights and recommendations.
5. Staying in touch: Keep in touch with the customer regularly, even if they do not have any current needs, to build and maintain a strong relationship.
6. Personalizing the interactions: Personalizing the interactions and taking into account the customer's specific needs and preferences, can help create a stronger bond between the customer and the IT company.
7. Keeping your promises and being accountable: Following through on your promises and being accountable for your actions is a key to building trust and credibility with customers.

By providing excellent customer service and continuously delivering value, you can build a long-term relationship with IT customers, which can lead to repeat business, positive word-of-mouth, and additional sales opportunities.

27 – What Is the Hidden Agenda in IT Business?

It's not uncommon for people or businesses to have hidden agendas in any industry, including the IT industry. A hidden agenda can refer to a goal or motive that is not openly stated or acknowledged. Some common examples of hidden agendas in the IT business might include:

- Seeking to gain a competitive advantage over others in the market

- Seeking to increase profits at the expense of the customer or other stakeholders
- Seeking to advance one's own career or reputation at the expense of others
- Seeking to influence or control the direction of a project or company

It's important to be aware of the possibility of hidden agendas, especially when making business decisions or working with others. It's always a good idea to be transparent and open about your own goals and motivations, and to try to understand the goals and motivations of others. This can help foster trust and collaboration and lead to more successful outcomes.

28 – What Is the Organizational Agenda of the Customer in IT Domain?

Customers in the IT domain may have various agendas, such as:

1. Finding the best solution: The customer may be looking for the best possible solution to their problem or pain point. They may be exploring multiple options and evaluating various vendors to find the most effective and efficient solution.
2. Maximizing ROI: The customer may be focused on maximizing their return on investment (ROI). They may be looking for a solution that provides the most value for their budget and delivers measurable results.

3. Improving efficiency: The customer may be looking for a solution that improves their efficiency and productivity. They may be interested in technology that streamlines their processes and reduces manual work.
4. Reducing costs: The customer may be looking for a solution that reduces their costs and improves their bottom line. They may be interested in technology that lowers their operational expenses or improves their profit margins.
5. Addressing compliance: The customer may be looking for a solution that helps them meet regulatory or compliance requirements. They may be interested in technology that ensures data security, privacy, or other compliance-related issues.

Overall, it is important to approach customers in the IT domain with an open mind and focus on understanding their needs, goals, and pain points. By building trust and credibility, and providing value, you can address their hidden agenda and ultimately close more deals.

29 – What Is the Personal Agenda of the Customer in IT Domain?

As an AI language model, I cannot determine the personal agenda of a customer in the IT domain. However, it is important to recognize that customers in the IT domain, like any other industry, may have personal agendas that influence their decision-making process. These personal agendas could include:

1. Advancing their career: The customer may be looking for a solution that helps them advance their career or gain recognition within their organization. They may be interested in technology that positions them as a thought leader or innovator.
2. Minimizing risk: The customer may be looking for a solution that minimizes their personal risk, such as avoiding a potential security breach or data loss. They may be interested in technology that ensures data privacy and security.
3. Addressing personal pain points: The customer may be looking for a solution that addresses their personal pain points or frustrations. They may be interested in technology that streamlines their work or simplifies their day-to-day tasks.
4. Building relationships: The customer may be interested in building relationships with vendors or partners who can support their personal and professional goals. They may be interested in technology that helps them network or collaborate with others.
5. Addressing personal bias: The customer may have personal biases that influence their decision-making process. They may have preferences for specific vendors or technologies based on personal experiences or relationships.

Overall, it is important to approach customers in the IT domain with an open mind and focus on understanding their needs, goals, and pain points. By building trust and credibility, and providing value, you can address their personal agenda and ultimately close more deals.

30 – How to Do a First Meeting with a Prospect in IT Domain?

1. Research the prospect and their company: Before the meeting, research the prospect and their company to gain a better understanding of their needs and pain points. This will help you tailor your pitch and proposal to their specific needs.
2. Prepare a clear agenda: Have a clear agenda for the meeting, including key points you want to discuss, questions you want to ask, and a specific call to action.
3. Communicate the value proposition: Clearly and concisely communicate the value of your product or service and how it addresses the prospect's specific needs. Use data and case studies to support your points.
4. Ask questions: Engage the prospect by asking questions and actively listening to their responses. This will help you gain a deeper understanding of their needs and concerns.
5. Address objections: Be prepared to address any objections or concerns the prospect may have. Provide examples and data to support your solution.
6. Next steps: Establish a clear next step or call to action for the prospect, such as setting up a follow-up meeting or providing a proposal.

7. Follow up: After the meeting, follow up with the prospect to provide additional information, answer any remaining questions, and move the process forward.

Overall, the first meeting with a prospect in the IT domain should be focused on building trust, understanding the prospects' needs and clearly communicating the value of your product or service to the prospects.

31 – What Types of Objections Customers Have in IT Domain?

Customers in the IT domain may have a variety of objections when considering a product or service. Some common objections include:

1. Cost: The customer may have concerns about the cost of the product or service, and may not see the value in paying the price.
2. Complexity: The customer may have concerns about the complexity of the solution and how it will integrate with their existing systems.
3. Risk: The customer may be worried about potential risks associated with the product or service, such as data security or scalability issues.
4. Timeframe: The customer may have concerns about the timeline for implementation or the availability of support.

5. Competitors: The customer may be considering other options and may have objections about the comparative value of your product or service.
6. No need: The customer may not see the need for the product or service at this time, or may not be aware of the benefits it can provide.
7. Lack of trust: The customer may not trust you or your company and may have objections based on past experiences or negative feedback.

It is important to be prepared to address these types of objections and to have solid arguments to overcome them, such as case studies, testimonials, and product demonstration.

32 – How to Handle Customer's Rejection as an IT Salesman?

It is normal to face rejection in sales, and it is important to learn how to handle it in a healthy and productive way. Here are some tips for handling customer rejection as an IT salesman:

1. Don't take it personally: Remember that customer rejection is not a reflection of your worth as a person. It may simply mean that the product or service you are offering is not a good fit for the customer at this time.
2. Use it as an opportunity to learn: Try to understand the reasons behind the customer's rejection. This can help you to improve your sales pitch and increase your chances of success in the future.

3. Keep a positive attitude: It can be difficult to maintain a positive attitude when faced with rejection, but it is important to stay professional and keep a positive outlook.
4. Don't give up: Don't let a single rejection discourage you. Instead, use it as motivation to work harder and improve your skills.
5. Move on: Once you have learned from the experience, it is important to move on and focus on the next opportunity. Dwelling on rejection can be counterproductive and prevent you from making progress.

33 – How to Respond to Customer's Objections in IT Domain?

Responding to customer objections in the IT domain can be done by following these steps:

1. Listen actively: Listen to the customer's objections and concerns, and show that you understand where they are coming from.
2. Acknowledge the objection: Acknowledge the customer's concerns and validate their feelings. Show them that you understand and empathize with their position.
3. Address the root cause: Identify the root cause of the objection and address it directly. Provide specific examples and data to support your solution.

4. Provide alternative solutions: If the customer has a valid concern, offer alternative solutions that address their needs while still meeting your own objectives.
5. Overcome with evidence: Use case studies, testimonials, and data to back up your claims and overcome objections.
6. Emphasize the benefits: Remind the customer of the benefits and value that your product or service will bring to their business.
7. End with a call to action: End the conversation with a clear call to action and set a specific follow-up date.
8. Address any doubts: Be prepared to provide the customer with any additional information or support they may need to make a decision.

By following these steps, you can effectively address customer objections in the IT domain, and increase the chances of closing the deal. It's also important to remember that not all objections are deal breakers, and some objections can be overcome with education, clear communication and evidence.

34 – What Are the Techniques for Handling Customer's Objections in IT Domain?

Handling customer objections is an important part of the IT sales process. Some techniques for handling objections in the IT domain include:

1. Listen actively: Listen to the customer's concerns and objections carefully and try to understand their perspective.
2. Acknowledge their concerns: Acknowledge the customer's concerns and validate them. This will help to build trust and show that you understand their perspective.
3. Ask questions: Ask open-ended questions to better understand the customer's needs and concerns. This will help you to address their objections more effectively.
4. Address their concerns directly: Address the customer's concerns directly and provide specific and relevant information that addresses their objections.
5. Provide evidence: Provide evidence and data to support your argument and demonstrate the value of your solution.
6. Use customer testimonials: Use customer testimonials and success stories to demonstrate the value and benefits of your solution.
7. Be transparent: Be transparent about any limitations or challenges of your solution and provide realistic and honest information.
8. Be patient: Be patient and take the time to address the customer's objections. Rushing or dismissing their concerns may lead to losing a potential sale.
9. Be flexible: Be flexible and willing to adapt to the customer's needs and requirements.
10. Follow-up: Follow-up with the customer after addressing their objections to ensure that they have been resolved and to maintain a positive relationship.

35 – What Are the Decision-Making Criteria?

Decision-making criteria refer to the specific factors that a customer will consider when making a decision to purchase a product or service. These can vary depending on the specific industry and product, but some common decision-making criteria for IT products and services include:

1. Functionality: The customer will consider whether the product or service meets their specific needs and can effectively solve their problems.
2. Price: The customer will consider the cost of the product or service and compare it to their budget and other options available in the market.
3. Quality: The customer will consider the quality of the product or service and whether it is reliable, durable, and fit for their purpose.
4. Support and Maintenance: The customer will consider the level of support and maintenance offered by the vendor, including warranties and service agreements.
5. Scalability: The customer will consider whether the product or service can scale to meet their changing needs and whether it will be able to grow with their business.
6. Integration: The customer will consider whether the product or service can be integrated seamlessly with their existing systems and infrastructure.
7. Security: The customer will consider the level of security offered by the product or service and whether it meets their specific security requirements.

8. Time to Deployment: The customer will consider the time required to implement the product or service and how it aligns with their business needs.
9. ROI: The customer will consider the Return on Investment (ROI) and how quickly they will see the benefits of the product or service.

Vendor reputation: The customer will consider the reputation of the vendor, including their track record of delivering quality products.

36 – Who Are the Decision-Influencers at the Customer Site in IT Domain?

In addition to the decision-makers, there are also decision influencers at customer sites in the IT domain. These are individuals or groups who may not have the final say in making a decision, but their opinions and feedback can influence the decision-making process. Here are some of the decision influencers in the IT domain:

1. Technical staff: Technical staff, such as IT engineers or developers, may provide technical input and recommendations to decision-makers.
2. Project managers: Project managers can help guide the decision-making process by providing project management expertise, timelines, and budgets.
3. End-users: End-users, such as employees or customers, can provide valuable feedback on how IT solutions will impact their day-to-day work.

4. Consultants: Consultants may be brought in to provide expert advice on specific IT solutions or projects.
5. Industry analysts: Industry analysts can provide insights into industry trends, emerging technologies, and vendor evaluations, which can influence decision-making.
6. Vendors: Vendors can provide product demonstrations, proofs of concept, and other information to help decision-makers evaluate IT solutions.
7. Regulators and Compliance Officers: Regulators and Compliance Officers can influence IT decision-making by setting standards and requirements that organizations must follow.

37 – Who Are the Decision-Makers at the Customer Site in IT Domain?

The decision-makers at a customer site in the IT domain can vary depending on the organization's size and structure, as well as the specific project or purchase involved. However, here are some of the most common decision-makers in the IT domain:

1. Chief Information Officer (CIO): The CIO is typically the highest-ranking IT executive in an organization and is responsible for setting the overall IT strategy and direction.
2. IT Director/Manager: The IT Director or Manager is responsible for overseeing the day-to-day operations

of the IT department, managing IT projects, and ensuring that IT initiatives align with the organization's goals.

3. IT Architects: IT Architects are responsible for designing and implementing IT systems that meet the organization's needs, including hardware, software, and network infrastructure.
4. IT Operations Manager: The IT Operations Manager is responsible for managing the ongoing operation and maintenance of the organization's IT systems, including hardware, software, and network infrastructure.
5. IT Security Manager: The IT Security Manager is responsible for ensuring the security and integrity of the organization's IT systems and data.
6. Business Leaders/Department Heads: Business leaders or department heads may also play a role in IT decision-making, particularly when IT initiatives are closely tied to specific business objectives.
7. End-Users: End-users of IT systems, such as employees or customers, may also provide input into IT decision-making, particularly when it comes to user experience and functionality.

Chapter 4

Opportunity's Sales Cycle

1 – Sales Process

The sales process in the IT domain typically involves several steps that are designed to identify, qualify, and close deals with potential customers. These steps include:

1. Prospecting: The process of identifying potential customers and creating a list of leads to target. This can be done through various means such as networking, online research, and marketing campaigns.
2. Qualifying: The process of determining which leads are most likely to become paying customers by assessing their needs, budget, and decision-making authority.
3. Presenting: The process of presenting the products or services to the potential customer and highlighting the value proposition, differentiators, and benefits of the solutions.

4. Handling objections: Anticipating and addressing any concerns or objections that the potential customer may have about the products or services.
5. Closing: The process of finalizing the deal and getting the customer to commit to purchasing the products or services.
6. Follow-up: The process of following up with the customer after the sale to ensure satisfaction and identify opportunities for upselling or cross-selling additional products or services.
7. Retention: The process of retaining customers by providing excellent customer service and encouraging repeat business.
8. Referral: The process of encouraging satisfied customers to refer others to your products or services, which can help drive new business and increase sales.

It's important to note that the sales process in the IT domain can be complex, and may involve a variety of different stakeholders and decision-makers. As a result, salespeople in the IT domain must be able to effectively communicate the value of their products or services to a range of different audiences and be able to handle complex objections and negotiations.

2 – Sales Funnel

The sales funnel in the IT domain is a model that describes the different stages that a potential customer goes through before making a purchase of an IT product or service. The funnel is typically divided into several stages, with each stage

representing a key step in the customer journey. The basic stages of the sales funnel in the IT domain are:
1. Awareness: At the top of the funnel, potential customers become aware of the IT product or service through various marketing channels, such as advertising, social media, search engines, or word-of-mouth.
2. Interest: In this stage, potential customers show an interest in the IT product or service by exploring more information about it, downloading a whitepaper or brochure, or attending a webinar or demo.
3. Consideration: This stage is where potential customers actively consider the IT product or service by comparing it to other similar solutions, asking questions, requesting a quote, or speaking with a sales representative.
4. Evaluation & Decision: After evaluating the IT product or service, potential customers make a decision whether or not to purchase it. This decision could be influenced by factors such as pricing, features, support, and reputation.
5. Purchase & Retention: After the purchase, the IT vendor provides ongoing support and maintenance to ensure the solution continues to meet the customer's needs. The customer may also provide feedback and recommendations to others.

By understanding the different stages of the sales funnel, IT companies can optimize their sales and marketing efforts to improve conversion rates and sales performance. They can use metrics such as conversion rates, click-through rates, and time spent at each stage of the funnel to identify areas of improvement and make data-driven decisions to optimize the sales funnel. Additionally, IT companies can use various tactics and strategies to guide potential customers through the different stages of the funnel, such as targeted content, email marketing, free trials or demos, or discounts and incentives.

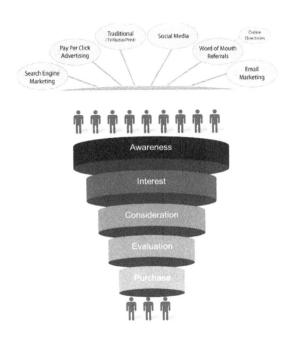

Sales Funnel

3 – Sales Cycle

The sales cycle in the IT domain typically refers to the process of selling and implementing technology solutions, software products, or IT services to clients. The length and complexity of the sales cycle can vary widely depending on the specific IT product or service being sold, the size and complexity of the organization being targeted, and the level of customization and integration required.

Here are the typical stages of the sales cycle in the IT domain:

1. Prospecting: This is the stage where the sales team identifies potential clients that may be interested in the IT solution or service being offered.
2. Needs analysis: In this stage, the sales team meets with the client to understand their specific requirements and business needs.
3. Solution design: Based on the client's requirements, the sales team works with technical experts to design a solution that meets their needs.
4. Proposal development: The sales team then creates a proposal that outlines the proposed solution, pricing, and other terms of the agreement.
5. Negotiation: At this stage, the sales team and the client negotiate the terms of the proposal and finalize the agreement.
6. Implementation: Once the agreement is signed, the implementation team begins the process of configuring and deploying the IT solution or service.
7. Support and maintenance: After implementation, the IT vendor provides ongoing support and maintenance to ensure the solution continues to meet the client's needs.

The sales cycle can take several weeks to several months depending on the complexity of the IT solution or service being sold, the size and complexity of the organization being targeted, and the level of customization and integration required.

4 – Lead Generation

The lead generation process in IT sales domain involves the steps a company takes to identify, attract, and convert potential customers into qualified leads. Here are the steps involved in the lead generation process:

1. Define your target audience: Identify your ideal customer profile, including their demographics, interests, pain points, and buying behavior.
2. Create a lead magnet: Develop a compelling offer, such as a free trial, demo, or whitepaper, to attract potential customers and capture their contact information.
3. Promote your lead magnet: Promote your offer through various channels, such as social media, email marketing, content marketing, and paid advertising, to attract potential customers to your website.
4. Capture leads: Use lead capture forms and landing pages to capture the contact information of potential customers who are interested in your offer.
5. Nurture leads: Develop a lead nurturing strategy to build relationships with your leads over time. Send them targeted and personalized messages with helpful information, relevant content, and offers that are tailored to their needs and interests.

6. Qualify leads: Evaluate your leads based on their fit and readiness to buy. Qualify them based on their budget, timeline, decision-making authority, and level of interest.
7. Pass leads to sales: Once a lead is qualified, pass it to your sales team for follow-up and further engagement. Ensure your sales team has the necessary information and context to have productive conversations with your leads.

Overall, the lead generation process in IT sales domain requires a strategic approach that combines various tactics and techniques to attract and convert potential customers into qualified leads. By consistently optimizing and measuring the effectiveness of your lead generation process, you can generate a steady flow of high-quality leads and increase your sales.

5 – How to Generate a Lead?

Generating leads is essential for any successful IT sales strategy. Here are some effective ways to generate leads in IT sales domain:

1. Referrals: Encourage your existing customers to refer you to their colleagues and friends who might be interested in your product or service.
2. Networking: Attend industry events, conferences, and trade shows to meet potential customers and build relationships with them.

3. Content marketing: Create and share valuable content, such as blog posts, whitepapers, and webinars, to attract potential customers to your website and generate leads.
4. Search engine optimization (SEO): Optimize your website and content for search engines to increase your visibility and attract organic traffic.
5. Email marketing: Build an email list of potential customers and send them targeted messages with information about your product or service.
6. Social media: Use social media platforms such as LinkedIn, Twitter, and Facebook to reach potential customers and engage with them.
7. Paid advertising: Invest in paid advertising, such as Google AdWords or LinkedIn Ads, to target specific audiences and generate leads.
8. Cold calling: Reach out to potential customers directly through cold calling or cold emailing, but make sure to follow best practices for these methods.

Overall, generating leads in IT sales domain requires a multi-faceted approach that combines various strategies tailored to your target audience and market. By consistently implementing these strategies and measuring their effectiveness, you can generate a steady stream of qualified leads and increase your sales.

6 – Here Are Some Tips for Making a Successful Sales Call to Your Lead:

1. Start the call with a strong introduction: Begin the call by introducing yourself and explaining the purpose of the call. This will help set the tone for the rest of the conversation.
2. Focus on the prospect's needs: During the call, focus on the prospect's needs and challenges. Ask questions to understand their needs and how your product or service can help solve their problems.
3. Use active listening: Pay attention to what the prospect is saying and use active listening techniques, such as repeating back what they have said or asking clarifying questions. This will help you better understand their needs and show that you are engaged in the conversation.
4. Tailor your message to the prospect: Customize your message to the specific needs and challenges of the prospect. This may involve highlighting specific features or benefits of your product or service that are most relevant to them.
5. Address objections: Anticipate and address any objections or concerns that the prospect may have about your product or service. This may involve providing additional information or resources to address their concerns.
6. End the call with a clear next step: At the end of the call, summarize the key points and determine a clear next step. This could be setting up a follow-up

meeting, sending additional information, or arranging a trial or demo of your product or service.

By following these tips, you can increase the chances of making a successful sales call and moving the prospect closer to a purchase.

7 – What Are the Active Listening Techniques?

Active listening techniques are essential in the IT domain as they help in effective communication and problem-solving. Here are some active listening techniques that can be applied in the IT domain:

1. Paraphrasing: This technique involves restating the speaker's words to confirm your understanding. It helps to clarify the meaning and ensure that you have correctly understood the speaker's message.
2. Asking open-ended questions: Open-ended questions encourage the speaker to provide more information, thereby helping to clarify the issue at hand. This technique also demonstrates your interest in the speaker's thoughts and ideas.
3. Reflecting feelings: Reflecting feelings involves acknowledging the speaker's emotions and demonstrating empathy. This technique helps to build trust and rapport and encourages the speaker to be more forthcoming with information.
4. Summarizing: Summarizing involves restating the speaker's main points to ensure that you have

understood the message. This technique also helps to organize the information and provides an opportunity to clarify any misunderstandings.
5. Nonverbal cues: Nonverbal cues, such as maintaining eye contact, nodding, and leaning forward, demonstrate your interest in the speaker and encourage them to continue speaking.
6. Active participation: Active participation involves engaging in the conversation and demonstrating your interest in the topic. This technique includes asking questions, providing feedback, and offering suggestions.

By using these active listening techniques in the IT domain, you can improve communication, resolve conflicts, and build stronger relationships with your colleagues and customers.

8 – How to Convert Leads to Prospects?

Converting leads into prospects is a crucial step in the sales process for any industry, including the IT domain. Here are some steps you can take to convert leads to prospects in the IT domain:

1. Understand your ideal customer profile: Before you start prospecting, you need to have a clear understanding of your ideal customer profile. This will help you identify the right leads to focus on and increase your chances of converting them into prospects.

2. Qualify your leads: Once you have identified your ideal customer profile, you need to qualify your leads to determine their level of interest and fit with your product or service. You can use various methods such as phone calls, emails, and social media to qualify leads.
3. Offer value: To convert leads into prospects, you need to offer them something of value. This could be a free trial, demo, or consultation. The goal is to provide them with a taste of your product or service and show them how it can benefit their business.
4. Follow up consistently: Following up consistently is essential to keep the conversation going and maintain interest. You can use various methods such as phone calls, emails, and social media to follow up with leads.
5. Personalize your communication: Personalizing your communication with leads can help you build a fruitful business relationship.

By following these steps, you can effectively convert leads into prospects in the IT domain and build lasting relationships with your customers.

9 – How to Evaluate the Prospects?

Evaluating prospects in IT sales domain involves identifying potential customers who are likely to be interested in your product or service and have a need for it. Here are some steps to evaluate prospects in IT sales domain:

1. Define your ideal customer: Develop a clear picture of your ideal customer, including their industry, company size, pain points, and business needs.
2. Research your target market: Conduct research to identify the companies that fit your ideal customer profile. You can use tools such as online directories, social media, and market research reports to find potential prospects.
3. Evaluate their needs: Once you have identified potential prospects, evaluate their needs and pain points. Determine how your product or service can solve their problems or help them achieve their business goals.
4. Understand their decision-making process: Analyze the decision-making process of your prospects to determine who the decision-makers are, what factors influence their decisions, and how long the sales cycle typically lasts.
5. Identify their budget: Determine whether your prospects have the budget to invest in your product or service. Understand their budgeting process and their financial constraints.
6. Analyze the competition: Analyze the competitive landscape to understand the strengths and weaknesses of your competitors. Determine how you can differentiate yourself from your competitors and add value to your prospects.
7. Establish trust: Building trust with your prospects is essential. Establish a relationship with them by providing helpful information, addressing their concerns, and following up regularly.

Overall, evaluating prospects in IT sales domain requires a thorough understanding of your target market, their needs, and the competitive landscape. By following these steps, you can identify the prospects with the highest potential and develop a strategy to convert them into customers.

10 – How to Convert Prospects into Opportunity?

Converting prospects into opportunities in the IT domain requires a strategic approach that focuses on building relationships, establishing trust, and demonstrating the value of your IT solutions. Here are some steps that you can follow to convert prospects into opportunities in the IT domain:

1. Identify the prospect's needs: Understand the prospect's pain points and requirements. This will help you tailor your sales pitch and demonstrate how your IT solutions can address their specific needs.
2. Demonstrate the value of your IT solutions: Provide a clear and compelling demonstration of how your IT solutions can help the prospect achieve their goals and solve their problems. Use case studies, testimonials, and other evidence to back up your claims.
3. Provide personalized solutions: Provide personalized solutions that meet the prospect's unique needs. Offer customized demos, product trials, and pricing options that align with their requirements.
4. Build trust and credibility: Build trust and credibility with the prospect by demonstrating your expertise in

the IT domain. Provide thought leadership content, share industry insights, and offer guidance on best practices in the IT industry.
5. Follow-up regularly: Follow up with the prospect regularly to keep them engaged and informed about your IT solutions. Address any concerns or questions they may have and provide additional information and resources as needed.
6. Provide excellent customer service: Provide excellent customer service to the prospect throughout the sales process. Respond promptly to their inquiries, be transparent about pricing and product features, and provide ongoing support after the sale is closed.

By following these steps, you can effectively convert prospects into opportunities in the IT domain and build long-term relationships with your customers.

11 – How to Evaluate the Opportunity?

Evaluating opportunities in IT sales domain can be challenging, but the following steps can help you to assess the potential of a sales opportunity in the IT industry:

1. Define the Opportunity: Start by defining the opportunity you are evaluating. Determine the type of product or service, the market size, the target audience, and the competition.
2. Understand the Market: Conduct market research to understand the current market trends, the needs and

pain points of the customers, and the competition in the market.

3. Determine the Potential ROI: Evaluate the potential return on investment (ROI) of the opportunity. Estimate the revenue potential, the cost of sales, and the expected profit margin.
4. Assess the Sales Process: Analyze the sales process and determine the resources required to close the sale. Evaluate the lead generation process, the sales cycle, and the sales funnel to determine the level of effort required to close the deal.
5. Determine the Sales Strategy: Develop a sales strategy that aligns with the opportunity. Determine the best approach to reach potential customers, communicate the value proposition, and close the deal.
6. Analyze the Risks: Identify the potential risks associated with the opportunity, including the competition, the market conditions, and the customer requirements. Determine how these risks can be mitigated.
7. Consider the Resources: Evaluate the resources required to pursue the opportunity, including the sales team, the marketing materials, and the technology infrastructure.

Overall, evaluating opportunities in IT sales domain requires a thorough understanding of the market, the competition, and the sales process. By following these steps, you can assess the potential of an opportunity and determine whether it is worth pursuing.

12 – How to Move the Opportunity into the Closing?

Moving an opportunity towards closing in the IT domain involves several steps. Here are some key steps you can follow:

1. Identify decision-makers: Determine who the decision-makers are and what their role is in the purchasing process. This will help you tailor your approach and messaging to their specific needs and interests.
2. Establish trust: Building trust with potential customers is essential in the IT domain. This can be done by providing case studies, testimonials, or references from existing customers, as well as by demonstrating expertise and knowledge.
3. Address objections: Identify potential objections or concerns that the customer may have and address them proactively. This can include pricing, implementation, or technical issues.
4. Provide a clear value proposition: Clearly articulate the value proposition of your product or service, and demonstrate how it can address the customer's specific pain points and needs.
5. Create a sense of urgency: Create a sense of urgency by highlighting the benefits of taking action now, such as cost savings, increased efficiency, or competitive advantage.
6. Offer incentives: Offer incentives, such as discounts or extended trial periods, to encourage the customer to make a decision.

7. Close the deal: Once the customer is ready to make a decision, be prepared to close the deal quickly and efficiently. This may involve finalizing contract terms, setting up payment arrangements, and coordinating implementation and training.

By following these steps, you can increase your chances of successfully moving an opportunity towards closing in the IT domain. However, it's important to keep in mind that the sales process can be complex and time-consuming, and may require multiple touchpoints and follow-up interactions before a deal is closed.

13 – What Is the Opportunity Sales Cycle Process?

The opportunity sales cycle process in IT sales domain refers to the steps involved in converting a qualified lead into a paying customer. Here are the stages typically involved in the opportunity sales cycle process:

1. Needs assessment: Conduct a thorough needs assessment to understand the prospect's pain points, business needs, and goals. Use this information to tailor your sales pitch and position your product or service as the solution.
2. Proposal: Create a detailed proposal that outlines how your product or service can solve the prospect's pain points and achieve their business goals. Include pricing, terms, and any other relevant details.

3. Demo/presentation: Provide a demo or presentation to showcase your product or service's features and benefits. Address any questions or objections the prospect may have.
4. Negotiation: Engage in negotiation with the prospect to reach a mutually beneficial agreement on pricing, terms, and other details.
5. Close: Once the prospect agrees to move forward, close the deal by finalizing the agreement, signing contracts, and receiving payment.
6. Onboarding: Work with the customer to onboard them and ensure a smooth transition to using your product or service. Provide training, support, and any necessary resources to help them achieve success.
7. Follow-up: Follow up with the customer after the sale to ensure their satisfaction and address any issues that may arise. Use this opportunity to build a long-term relationship and potentially upsell or cross-sell additional products or services.

Overall, the opportunity sales cycle process in IT sales domain requires a consultative and strategic approach that focuses on understanding the prospect's needs, providing value, and building trust. By effectively managing the opportunity sales cycle process, you can increase your conversion rate, generate more revenue, and build a loyal customer base.

14 – Don't Do the Common Mistakes During the Sales Process

There are several common mistakes that sales professionals can make during the IT sales process. Here are a few examples:

1. Failing to fully understand the customer's needs: It's important to take the time to fully understand the customer's needs and challenges before presenting a solution. If you don't fully understand their needs, it will be difficult to show how your solution can meet those needs.
2. Being too pushy or aggressive: It's important to be persistent in following up with leads, but it's also important to respect the customer's time and boundaries. Being too pushy or aggressive can turn off potential customers and damage your relationship with them.
3. Failing to tailor the presentation to the customer: Customizing the presentation to the customer's specific needs and interests is crucial to persuading them to make a purchase. If the presentation is not tailored to their needs, they may not see the value in the solution.
4. Not handling objections effectively: Objections are a normal part of the sales process, and it's important to be prepared to handle them effectively. This includes listening to the customer's concerns, addressing them in a respectful manner, and showing how the solution can meet their needs.

5. Not following up after the sale: It's important to follow up with the customer after the sale to ensure that they are satisfied with the solution and to identify any potential issues. Failing to follow up can lead to lost opportunities for repeat business and referrals.

Overall, avoiding these common mistakes can help sales professionals effectively navigate the IT sales process and achieve success.

15 – What Is the Sales Opportunity Assessment Tool?

A sales opportunity assessment tool in the IT domain is a method or technique used to evaluate the potential of a sales opportunity and determine the likelihood of closing a sale.

It can take many forms, such as a scorecard, a questionnaire or a template that sales representatives can use to evaluate potential opportunities. It typically includes a set of criteria or factors that are used to assess the potential of the opportunity.

These criteria can include factors such as:

- The customer's needs and pain points
- The customer's budget and willingness to invest
- The customer's decision-making process and key stakeholders
- The competition and current vendor relationships
- The timeline and urgency of the opportunity
- The potential revenue that could be generated

The sales opportunity assessment tool can be used to assign scores or ratings to each of these criteria, and then combine them to determine an overall score or rating for the opportunity. This score can then be used to prioritize opportunities and allocate resources accordingly.

It's important to note that sales opportunity assessment tool should be regularly reviewed, updated and tailored to the specific needs of the organization and the IT domain.

16 – What Are the Sales Opportunity Evaluation Criteria?

There are several key criteria that can be used to evaluate sales opportunities in the IT domain. Here are some common ones:

1. Business fit: This refers to whether the solution being sold aligns with the client's business objectives and needs. A good sales opportunity should address a specific pain point or help the client achieve a particular goal.
2. Budget: The client's budget is a critical factor in evaluating a sales opportunity. If the solution is too expensive for the client, then it may not be a viable opportunity.
3. Decision-making process: Understanding the client's decision-making process is important. If the sales process is too complicated or involves too many decision-makers, then it may be difficult to close the deal.

4. Competition: The level of competition in the market is an important consideration. If there are many other solutions available that address the same problem, then the opportunity may be less attractive.
5. Implementation complexity: If the solution requires a significant amount of effort to implement, then it may be less appealing to the client. Solutions that can be easily integrated into existing systems are generally more attractive.
6. ROI: The return on investment (ROI) is an important factor to consider. Clients want to see that the solution will provide a tangible benefit that justifies the cost
7. Vendor credibility: The credibility of the vendor is an important consideration. Clients are more likely to buy from vendors with a proven track record of success.

By evaluating sales opportunities based on these criteria, IT companies can identify the most promising opportunities and focus their sales efforts accordingly.

17 – Negotiation Strategies in IT Domain

Negotiation skills refer to the ability to effectively communicate and reach an agreement with others, typically in a business setting. Good negotiation skills involve being able to identify and prioritize your own interests, as well as being able to understand and consider the interests of the other party. Here are some specific techniques that can help improve negotiation skills:

1. Identify your goals: Before entering into a negotiation, it's important to identify your goals and priorities. This will help you stay focused and ensure that you get what you need from the negotiation.
2. Research and prepare: Gathering as much information as possible about the other party and the negotiation itself can help you better understand their interests and needs, as well as identify potential areas of compromise.
3. Communicate effectively: Good communication is key to successful negotiation. This includes being able to clearly articulate your interests and needs, as well as actively listening and considering the interests of the other party.
4. Find common ground: Look for areas where your interests overlap with those of the other party, and try to find ways to meet both parties' needs.
5. Be flexible: Be willing to compromise and consider alternative options. This can help you find solutions that work for both parties.

Overall, negotiation skills are important because they enable you to effectively reach agreements with others, whether in business or in other settings. By practicing good negotiation skills, you can improve your ability to effectively communicate and collaborate with others.

18 – What Are the Effective Communication and Negotiation Skills?

Effective communication and negotiation skills are critical in the IT sales process. Some key skills include:

1. Active listening: Being able to listen actively and understand the customer's needs and concerns is important in order to offer relevant solutions and build trust.
2. Clear and concise communication: Being able to communicate clearly and concisely is essential in order to ensure that the customer understands your message and to avoid confusion or misunderstandings.
3. Persuasion: Being able to persuade the customer that your solution is the best fit for their needs is important in order to close the sale.
4. Empathy: Being able to understand and relate to the customer's perspective and needs is important in order to build a positive relationship and gain their trust.
5. Problem-solving: Being able to identify and solve problems is important in order to offer relevant solutions and provide value to the customer.
6. Adaptability: Being able to adapt to the customer's needs and changing circumstances is important in order to remain responsive and relevant.
7. Conflict resolution: Being able to effectively manage and resolve conflicts is important in order to maintain a positive relationship and close the sale.

8. Negotiation: Being able to negotiate effectively with the customer is important in order to reach mutually beneficial agreements and close the sale.
9. Time management: Being able to effectively manage your time and prioritize tasks is important in order to meet deadlines and keep the sales process moving forward.
10. Presentation skills: Being able to effectively present your solutions and products to the customer is important in order to demonstrate their value and close the sale.

19 – What Are the Negotiation Terminologies?

Negotiation terminologies are the specific terms and phrases used in the process of negotiating an agreement between two or more parties. Here are some common negotiation terminologies:

1. BATNA (Best Alternative to a Negotiated Agreement): The alternative option available to a party if the negotiation fails to reach an agreement.
2. Concession: An offer or compromise made by one party to the other during the negotiation process.
3. Counteroffer: A response to an initial offer that proposes different terms or conditions.
4. Deadlock: A situation in which the parties are unable to reach an agreement due to a fundamental disagreement or impasse.

5. Good Faith: The requirement for each party to act honestly and fairly during the negotiation process.
6. Interests: The underlying needs, goals, and concerns of each party that motivate their negotiation positions.
7. Reservation Price: The lowest price or highest cost that a party is willing to accept in a negotiation.
8. Win-Win: A negotiation outcome that satisfies the interests and needs of both parties, resulting in a mutually beneficial agreement.
9. ZOPA (Zone of Possible Agreement): The range of options and terms that could potentially satisfy both parties in a negotiation.
10. Walkaway Point: The point at which a party decides to end the negotiation and pursue their BATNA instead.

20 – What Is the Decoy in IT Negotiation Domain?

In the context of negotiation, a decoy is a tactic used to influence the perception or decision-making of the other party by presenting them with a less attractive option than the one being offered. In the IT negotiation domain, decoys may be used to manipulate the other party's preferences or perceptions and improve the chances of reaching a favorable agreement. Here are some examples of decoys that may be used in IT negotiation:

1. Feature-Decoy: A feature-decoy involves presenting a less desirable product or service option alongside a

more expensive or desirable option. This tactic is used to make the more expensive option seem more appealing by comparison. For example, a software vendor may offer two versions of their product, one with basic features and a lower price, and another with more advanced features at a higher price.
2. Price-Decoy: A price-decoy involves presenting a higher-priced option alongside a more affordable option. This tactic is used to make the more affordable option seem like a better value by comparison. For example, a vendor may offer three versions of a software product, one with basic features at a low price, a second with advanced features at a higher price, and a third with additional features at an even higher price.
3. Time-Decoy: A time-decoy involves setting an expiration date on an offer or deadline for a decision. This tactic is used to create a sense of urgency and pressure the other party into making a decision. For example, a vendor may offer a discount on a software product for a limited time only.
4. Authority-Decoy: An authority-decoy involves introducing a third-party authority figure or expert to influence the other party's decision-making. This tactic is used to lend credibility to the negotiation position or proposal. For example, a vendor may bring in a consultant or industry expert to support their claims or pricing strategy.

It is important to be aware of decoy tactics and to critically evaluate all offers and proposals in a negotiation to ensure that the terms and conditions are fair and reasonable.

21 – How to Negotiate Effectively in IT Domain?

Effective negotiation in the IT domain involves several key elements:

1. Research: Gather as much information as possible about the topic of negotiation, including market trends, industry standards, and the specific needs and priorities of the other party.
2. Preparation: Develop a clear and well-reasoned argument for your position, and anticipate potential objections or counterarguments from the other party
3. Communication: Communicate your argument in a clear and persuasive manner, using facts and data to support your position.
4. Flexibility: Be open to compromise and willing to find creative solutions that meet the needs of both parties.
5. Follow-up: After the negotiation, be sure to follow up with the other party to ensure that the agreement is being implemented as agreed.
6. Empathy: Try to put yourself in the other party's shoes, and understand their perspective.
7. Focus on Interests, not positions: Try to understand the underlying interests of the other party, and look

for ways to satisfy those interests while still meeting your own needs.

22 – What Is the Preparation Before Negotiation in IT Domain?

Before entering into a negotiation in the IT domain, it's important to prepare by:

1. Researching the topic: Gather as much information as possible about the specific area of negotiation, including market trends, industry standards, and the specific needs and priorities of the other party.
2. Identifying your goals and objectives: Clearly define what you hope to achieve through the negotiation and what you are willing to compromise on.
3. Developing a strategy: Create a plan of action that outlines the steps you will take during the negotiation and how you will respond to different scenarios.
4. Identifying potential objections: Anticipate any objections or counterarguments the other party may have, and prepare responses in advance.
5. Identifying your BATNA (Best Alternative To a Negotiated Agreement): Determine your best alternative course of action if the negotiation is unsuccessful, so you can walk away if you have to.
6. Gather data and facts: Collect data and facts that support your position and can be used to justify your proposed terms.

7. Practice: Rehearse your arguments, delivery, and responses to objections to be more comfortable and confident during the negotiation.
8. Understand the other party's perspective: Try to understand the other party's motivations, priorities, and constraints in order to identify potential areas of compromise.

23 – What Is Win-Win Negotiation Strategy?

A "win-win" negotiation strategy in the IT domain is one in which both parties feel that they have achieved a positive outcome. This type of negotiation is based on the idea that both parties can benefit from a mutually beneficial agreement, rather than one party winning at the expense of the other.

Some key elements of a win-win negotiation strategy in the IT domain include:

1. Identifying shared goals: Look for areas of common ground and opportunities for both parties to achieve their desired outcomes.
2. Creating options: Generate a range of potential solutions that can meet the needs of both parties.
3. Focusing on interests, not positions: Try to understand the underlying interests of the other party and look for ways to satisfy those interests while still meeting your own needs.
4. Communicating openly and honestly: Share information and express your concerns and priorities in a transparent and candid way.

5. Building trust: Foster a positive and collaborative relationship with the other party to build trust and establish a foundation for future negotiations.
6. Being flexible: Be open to compromise and willing to find creative solutions that meet the needs of both parties.
7. Seeking mutually beneficial agreements: Look for ways to create agreements that benefit both parties and avoid zero-sum solutions in which one party wins at the expense of the other.
8. Long-term perspective: Consider the long-term relationship with the other party and how the agreement will affect future interactions and negotiations.

24 – What Are the Negotiation Strategies in IT Domain?

There are several negotiation strategies that can be used in the IT domain, including:

1. Competitive: A competitive strategy involves taking a hardline stance and trying to get the best deal possible for yourself, regardless of the other party's needs. This strategy can be effective when you have a strong bargaining position and are dealing with a less experienced negotiator.
2. Collaborative: A collaborative strategy involves working with the other party to find a solution that meets the needs of both parties. This strategy is often used in situations where a long-term relationship is

important and both parties have something to gain from a mutually beneficial agreement.
3. Accommodative: An accommodative strategy involves being willing to make concessions in order to reach an agreement. This strategy is often used when the other party has more power or when maintaining a relationship is more important than getting the best deal.
4. Compromise: A compromise strategy involves finding a middle ground that both parties can accept, even if neither party gets exactly what they want. This strategy is often used when both parties have some flexibility and are willing to make concessions.
5. Avoiding: An avoiding strategy involves postponing or avoiding the negotiation altogether, usually when the issue at hand is not important enough to warrant the effort and potential damage to the relationship.
6. Problem Solving: A problem solving strategy is a win-win strategy, where both parties work together to find a mutually beneficial solution that addresses both party's needs and concerns.

Ultimately, the most effective strategy will depend on the specific circumstances of the negotiation and your goals and objectives.

25 – What Are the Negotiation Techniques?

There are several negotiation techniques that can be used in the IT domain, including:

1. Active Listening: Pay close attention to what the other party is saying and ask clarifying questions to ensure you understand their perspective.
2. Questioning: Ask open-ended questions to gather information and understand the other party's needs and priorities.
3. Summarizing: Repeat back key points to confirm your understanding and ensure that both parties are on the same page.
4. Reflecting Emotions: Acknowledge the other party's emotions and show that you understand their perspective.
5. Assertive communication: Clearly express your needs, wants, and concerns while being respectful of the other party.
6. Empathy: Put yourself in the other party's shoes and try to understand their perspective, priorities and constraints.
7. Brainstorming: Generate a wide range of potential solutions and options that can meet the needs of both parties.
8. Anchoring: Establishing the initial price, terms, or position as the starting point for the negotiation, and then adjusting it as needed.
9. BATNA: Identify your best alternative course of action if the negotiation is unsuccessful, so you can walk away if you have to.
10. ZOPA (zone of possible agreement): Identify the range of possible agreements that would be acceptable to both parties, and work within that range to find a mutually beneficial solution.

11. Closing the deal: Once agreement has been reached, finalize the deal by summarizing the key terms and getting the commitment from both parties.

26 – What Are the Negotiation Tactics?

There are many negotiation tactics that can be used to achieve a desired outcome. Here are some common tactics used in negotiations:

1. Anchoring: Setting an initial offer or position that serves as a starting point for the negotiation.
2. Good cop, bad cop: A tactic where one negotiator takes a hardline stance while the other takes a more conciliatory approach.
3. Limited authority: Pretending to have less authority or decision-making power than you actually do.
4. Time pressure: Creating a sense of urgency to close the deal.
5. Walkaway: Being willing to walk away from the negotiation if your terms are not met.
6. BATNA (Best Alternative to a Negotiated Agreement): Knowing your walkaway point or the best alternative you have if the negotiation falls through.
7. ZOPA (Zone of Possible Agreement): Knowing the range of concessions you are willing to make and where the other party's interests lie.
8. Concession: Making small concessions to build trust and move the negotiation forward.

9. Persuasion: Using evidence, logic and emotional appeals to influence the other party.
10. Active listening: Paying close attention to the other party's words and nonverbal cues to understand their perspective.

It's important to note that some of these tactics can be seen as manipulative and unethical if used in a deceitful way. It is important to use these tactics in a fair and transparent manner and to consider the long-term relationship with the other party.

27 – How to Negotiate Positively?

1. Start by clearly defining the issue at hand and your desired outcome.
2. Understand the other party's perspective and interests.
3. Look for common ground and areas of compromise.
4. Use "I" statements to express your own needs and concerns, rather than blaming or accusing the other party.
5. Avoid making demands or ultimatums.
6. Remain flexible and open to new ideas and solutions.
7. Focus on the future and finding a mutually beneficial solution.
8. Communicate effectively and actively listen to the other party.
9. If necessary, seek the help of a neutral third-party mediator.

10. Be willing to walk away if the negotiation is not beneficial for both parties.

28 – What Are the Competition Terminologies?

There are several competition terminologies used in the IT domain. Some of the commonly used ones include:

1. Market share: The percentage of total sales of a particular product or service that a company has within a specific market.
2. Competitive analysis: An assessment of the strengths and weaknesses of a company's competitors, as well as the opportunities and threats posed by those competitors.
3. Differentiation: The process of creating a unique product or service that sets a company apart from its competitors.
4. Price wars: A situation where competitors engage in a series of price cuts in an attempt to gain market share.
5. Customer retention: The ability of a company to keep its existing customers from switching to a competitor
6. Brand awareness: The extent to which consumers are aware of a company's brand and associate it with a particular product or service.
7. Innovation: The process of developing new products or services that offer unique features or benefits compared to those of competitors.

8. Sales funnel: The stages through which potential customers pass before making a purchase, from initial awareness to the final purchase decision.
9. SWOT analysis: An assessment of a company's strengths, weaknesses, opportunities, and threats, which helps identify areas where the company can improve its competitive position.
10. Value proposition: The unique combination of benefits that a company offers to its customers, which sets it apart from its competitors.

29 – What Is the Competitive Analysis?

Competitive analysis is a process of identifying and evaluating the strengths and weaknesses of your company's competitors in the same market or industry. The objective of competitive analysis is to understand the competitive landscape, identify areas of opportunity, and develop effective strategies to outperform your competitors.

Competitive analysis typically involves the following steps:

1. Identify your competitors: The first step in competitive analysis is to identify your competitors in the market. This includes both direct and indirect competitors who offer similar products or services to your target customers.
2. Collect information: Collect information on your competitors' products, services, marketing strategies, sales tactics, pricing, distribution channels, and customer feedback. This can be done through various

methods such as surveys, online research, customer feedback, and social media monitoring.
3. Analyze the data: Once you have collected the information, analyze it to identify your competitors' strengths and weaknesses, including their unique selling points, target audience, market share, pricing strategies, and marketing channels.
4. Develop strategies: Based on your analysis, develop effective strategies to improve your competitive position in the market. This may involve improving your product or service, offering better pricing, expanding your distribution channels, or enhancing your marketing strategies.
5. Monitor and adjust: Finally, monitor the effectiveness of your strategies and adjust them as needed based on changes in the market or your competitors' actions.

Competitive analysis is an ongoing process that should be regularly reviewed and updated to stay ahead of your competitors in the market.

Attributes	Competitor A	Competitor B	Competitor C
Price			
Quality			
Customer Service			
Reputation			
Location			

Competitive Analysis

30 – What Is the SWOT Analysis?

SWOT analysis is a strategic planning tool used to identify and evaluate the Strengths, Weaknesses, Opportunities, and Threats of a company or project. The analysis provides a framework for understanding the internal and external factors that affect the success of a business or initiative.

The strengths and weaknesses refer to internal factors, such as the company's resources, capabilities, and processes. Opportunities and threats are external factors, such as economic trends, regulatory changes, and competitive pressures.

SWOT analysis is typically used to develop a business strategy or to evaluate a new product or service. By understanding its strengths and weaknesses, a company can identify areas where it needs to improve or invest. By evaluating opportunities and threats, a company can identify new markets, potential partnerships, or areas where it needs to mitigate risks.

The SWOT analysis can be presented in a matrix format, with the strengths and weaknesses listed in the top row, and opportunities and threats listed in the bottom row. Each quadrant of the matrix represents a different combination of internal and external factors and can be used to guide strategic decision-making. By conducting a SWOT analysis, IT companies can gain insights into their strengths and weaknesses, identify areas for improvement, and take advantage of opportunities while mitigating threats. This information can help them make strategic decisions about product development, marketing, and resource allocation.

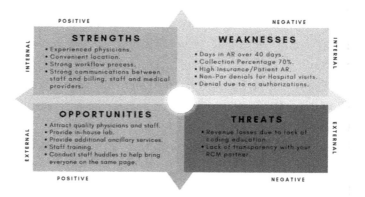

SWOT Analysis

31 – How to Handle the Competition as an IT Salesperson?

Competition is a normal part of the sales process, and it can be helpful to stay informed about what other companies or salespeople are offering. Here are a few strategies for handling competition as an IT salesperson:

1. Know your product: Make sure you have a thorough understanding of your own products or services, and be prepared to explain how they are different from or better than the competition.
2. Know your customer: Understand the needs and concerns of your customers, and be prepared to address any objections they may have about your product versus a competitor's.
3. Differentiate yourself: Look for ways to stand out from the competition, such as by offering unique

features or services, or by providing excellent customer service.
4. Stay up-to-date: Keep track of industry trends and any new products or services being offered by competitors.
5. Focus on your strengths: Don't try to compete on every front, but instead focus on the areas where you excel and where you can offer the most value to your customers.

By following these strategies, you can effectively compete in the marketplace and achieve success as an IT salesperson.

32 – What Are the Competition Strategies?

There are several strategies that IT companies can use to compete in the market. Some of the main competition strategies include:

1. Differentiation: Offering unique or superior products or services that distinguish the company from its competitors. This can be achieved through technological innovation, superior quality, or exceptional customer service.
2. Niche marketing: Focusing on a specific market segment or niche that is not well-served by competitors. This allows the company to gain a foothold in the market and establish a loyal customer base.

3. Cost leadership: Focusing on reducing costs in order to offer lower prices than competitors. This can be achieved through economies of scale, efficient operations, or a lower cost structure.
4. Branding and marketing: Building a strong brand and marketing the company's products and services effectively can help to create a positive image and differentiate the company from competitors.
5. Strategic partnerships and alliances: Forming strategic partnerships and alliances with other companies can help to expand the company's reach and increase its resources.
6. Innovation: Continuously developing new and improved products, services and features can help to stay ahead of the competition.
7. Personalized services: Offering customized and tailored services for different customers can help to build a strong relationship with the customers.
8. Building trust: Building trust and credibility with customers is essential in IT sales. Salespeople must be able to demonstrate their knowledge and expertise in the field, and build a relationship of trust with their customers.
9. Understanding the customers' pain points: Understanding the customers' pain points, offering solutions to them and addressing their concerns can help to win their trust and loyalty.
10. Keeping an eye on the competition: Keeping an eye on the competition, understanding their strengths and weaknesses and adapting accordingly can help to stay ahead in the game.

33 – How to Attack Competition?

Competing in the IT domain can be challenging, but there are a few strategies you can use to gain an advantage over your competitors:

1. Offer unique and innovative products or services: Develop products or services that offer unique features and benefits that your competitors don't have. Be sure to keep up with the latest trends in technology to ensure that you're providing cutting-edge solutions to your customers.
2. Build a strong brand: Invest in building a strong brand that resonates with your target audience. Your brand should convey your unique value proposition and differentiate you from your competitors.
3. Provide exceptional customer service: Focus on providing outstanding customer service to your clients. This can help you build strong relationships with your customers, which can lead to repeat business and referrals.
4. Focus on your niche: Instead of trying to be everything to everyone, focus on a specific niche in the IT domain. By specializing in a particular area, you can become known as the go-to provider in that area and establish a reputation for expertise.
5. Leverage social media: Use social media to connect with your audience, share valuable content, and promote your brand. By building a strong social media presence, you can increase your visibility and engage with your customers on a regular basis.

6. Keep an eye on your competitors: Monitor your competitors' activities, including their products, pricing, and marketing strategies. This can help you identify gaps in the market and opportunities for differentiation.
7. Continuously innovate and improve: Continuously evaluate your products, services, and processes to identify areas for improvement. By staying ahead of the curve and continually innovating, you can stay competitive and differentiate yourself from the competition.

34 – How to Team-Up with My Competitor?

Teaming up with a competitor in the IT domain can be a strategic move that can benefit both parties. Here are some steps that you can follow:

1. Identify common goals: Look for areas where you and your competitor have common interests, such as developing a new technology, penetrating a new market, or reducing costs. This will provide a strong foundation for collaboration.
2. Reach out to your competitor: Contact your competitor and express your interest in working together. Be clear about the benefits that you envision for both parties.
3. Establish clear boundaries: Set clear boundaries around what each party will be responsible for and what each party can expect from the other. This will

help to avoid misunderstandings and ensure that both parties are on the same page.
4. Define the scope of the collaboration: Identify specific projects or initiatives that you will be working on together. Define the scope of the collaboration, including timelines, milestones, and deliverables.
5. Establish a legal agreement: It's important to have a legal agreement in place that outlines the terms of the collaboration. This should include issues such as intellectual property rights, confidentiality, and dispute resolution.
6. Communicate effectively: Effective communication is essential for a successful collaboration. Establish regular communication channels and keep your competitor updated on progress and any issues that arise.
7. Monitor and evaluate the collaboration: Regularly monitor the collaboration to ensure that it is meeting the goals that were established at the outset. Evaluate the collaboration periodically to identify areas for improvement and make any necessary adjustments.

Remember, teaming up with a competitor can be a win-win situation for both parties if done correctly. It requires trust, clear communication, and a shared vision for success.

35 – What Are the Competition Techniques?

There are several techniques that IT companies can use to compete in the market. Some of the main competition techniques include:

1. Competitive Intelligence: Gathering information about the competition and their products, services, pricing, marketing, and distribution strategies.
2. Benchmarking: Comparing the company's performance to that of its competitors in order to identify areas of improvement.
3. Market Segmentation: Identifying and targeting specific segments of the market that are not well-served by competitors.
4. Product positioning: Positioning the company's products or services in a way that differentiates them from those of competitors.
5. Pricing strategies: Developing pricing strategies that are competitive and attractive to customers.
6. Promotion: Developing and executing effective marketing and advertising campaigns to promote the company's products and services.
7. Sales and Distribution: Developing and implementing effective sales and distribution strategies to reach customers and increase market share.
8. Customer Relationship Management: Building and maintaining strong relationships with customers through personalized service, follow-up, and loyalty programs.

9. Innovation: Continuously developing new and improved products, services, and features can help to stay ahead of the competition.
10. Collaboration: Collaborating with other companies and organizations to create joint ventures, partnerships, and alliances to gain access to new resources and customers.
11. Digital marketing: Utilizing digital marketing channels such as social media, search engine optimization, email marketing, and online advertising to reach and engage with customers.
12. Providing free trials: Offering free trials of the products or services can help the customers to try and experience the product before purchasing it.
13. Building a strong online presence: Building a strong online presence by creating a professional website, developing a blog and being active on social media can help to increase brand awareness and attract potential customers.
14. Creating a referral program: Creating a referral program can help to attract new customers through word-of-mouth marketing.

36 – Changing the Ground Rules?

There are several competition techniques that can be used in the IT industry that involve changing the ground rules of the competition. Some of these techniques include:

1. Disruptive Innovation: Introducing new technologies or business models that disrupt existing market dynamics and create new opportunities for growth.
2. Redefining the market: Redefining the market by creating new categories, segments or redefining the existing ones, so that the company's products or services are the best fit.
3. Creating new distribution channels: Creating new distribution channels, such as online marketplaces, that can help to reach new customers and increase market share.
4. Developing new partnerships: Developing new partnerships with companies, organizations, or individuals that can help to increase the reach of the company's products or services.
5. Creating a new pricing model: Creating a new pricing model, such as a subscription-based or pay-as-you-go model, that can help to increase revenue and customer loyalty.
6. Leveraging digital platforms: Leveraging digital platforms and technologies, such as AI, IoT, and cloud computing, to create new products, services and revenue streams.
7. Creating a new customer experience: Creating a new customer experience by using technology, design, and personalization to create a unique and engaging experience for customers.
8. Creating a new brand: Creating a new brand, or rebranding, to improve the company's image, increase customer loyalty and attract new customers.

9. Creating a new business model: Creating a new business model, such as a freemium, licensing, or subscription-based model, that can help to increase revenue and customer loyalty.
10. Creating a new distribution model: Creating a new distribution model, such as a direct-to-consumer or online-only model, that can help to increase revenue and reach new customers.

By changing the ground rules of the competition, companies can create new opportunities for growth, increase revenue and market share, and gain a competitive edge in the IT industry.

37 − Closing Deal in IT Domain:

Sales closing in the IT domain refers to the final step in the sales process where the salesperson asks for the customer's commitment to purchase the product or service being offered. The goal of closing is to secure a sale and bring the sale process to a successful conclusion.

Change the "Always Be Closing" to the "Always Be Helping."

Closing in IT domain can be achieved by building trust and understanding with the potential client, clearly communicating the value of your product or service, and addressing any concerns or objections they may have. It is also important to establish a clear and specific next step or call to action, such as setting up a follow-up meeting or signing a contract. Additionally, building a strong relationship and maintaining good communication throughout the sales process can help increase the likelihood of closing the deal.

It's important to note that closing a sale in IT domain also involves understanding the customer's specific needs and pain points, and tailoring the sales pitch accordingly. It also involves providing relevant and useful information to the customer, this will help establish credibility, build trust and increase the likelihood of closing a deal. Additionally, building a relationship with the customer and establishing trust can increase the likelihood of future sales opportunities.

Closing in IT domain can involve different techniques and strategies, such as the "Assumptive Close," "Alternative Close," "Summary Close," "Trial Close" and "Objection Close" among others. These techniques are used to address customer objections, overcome any remaining concerns or questions, and ultimately secure the sale.

In the IT domain, closing a sale can also involve negotiating the terms of the sale, such as the price, payment terms, and delivery schedule.

38 – What Are the Closing Techniques?

There are different types of closing techniques used by salespeople to close a sale in the IT domain. Here's a brief description of each:

1. **Assumptive Close:** In an assumptive close, the salesperson assumes that the customer has already made a decision to buy the product or service. The salesperson may use language like "When would you like us to deliver the product?" or "How would you

like to pay for the service?" This technique is best used when the customer has shown strong interest in the product or service.

2. **Alternative Close:** In an alternative close, the salesperson presents the customer with two options, both of which lead to a sale. For example, the salesperson may say "Would you like to purchase the basic package or the premium package?" This technique is effective because it gives the customer a sense of control and can help to overcome objections.

3. **Summary Close:** In a summary close, the salesperson summarizes the benefits of the product or service and asks for the sale. For example, the salesperson may say "So, based on what we've discussed today, it seems like our product would be a good fit for your needs. Would you like to move forward with the purchase?" This technique is effective because it reminds the customer of the benefits of the product or service.

4. **Trial Close:** In a trial close, the salesperson asks the customer for a small commitment, such as trying the product or service for a limited time, before asking for a larger commitment. For example, "Would you be willing to try our software for a free trial period before committing to a purchase?"

5. **Objection Close:** In an objection close, the salesperson addresses the customer's objections and tries to overcome them. For example, the salesperson may say "I understand your concern about the price, but let me show you how our product can save you money in the long run." This technique is effective

because it shows the customer that the salesperson is listening to their concerns and is willing to work with them to find a solution.

6. **The Urgency Close:** This technique involves creating a sense of urgency or scarcity to motivate the customer to make a decision. For example, "Our current promotion ends within 20 days, so if you don't buy now, you'll miss out on the discount."

These are just a few of the different closing techniques that can be used in the IT domain. It's important for salespeople to be flexible and adapt their approach based on the specific needs and preferences of each customer.

39 – What Are the Closing Deal Terminologies?

Closing deal terminologies in the IT domain refer to the final stages of a sales negotiation between a company and its potential customer. The following are some of the commonly used closing deal terminologies in the IT domain:

1. **Contract signing:** This refers to the act of signing a legally binding agreement between the company and its customer. The contract outlines the terms and conditions of the sale, including the product or service being purchased, the price, delivery date, and any warranties or guarantees.

2. **Purchase order:** A purchase order is a document issued by the customer to the company that confirms the details of the sale, including the product or service being purchased, the quantity, and the price. Once the

company receives the purchase order, they can proceed with fulfilling the order.
3. **Acceptance testing:** Acceptance testing is a process where the customer tests the product or service to ensure it meets their requirements and specifications. Once the customer approves the product or service, the sale is considered closed.
4. **Delivery and acceptance:** This refers to the process of delivering the product or service to the customer and the customer accepting the delivery. Once the customer accepts the delivery, the sale is considered closed.
5. **Payment and invoicing:** Payment and invoicing refer to the process of invoicing the customer for the product or service and receiving payment from the customer. Once the payment is received, the sale is considered closed.

Closing deal terminologies in the IT domain can vary depending on the type of product or service being sold and the specific terms and conditions of the sale. It's important for both the company and the customer to carefully review and understand the closing deal terminologies before finalizing the sale.

40 – What Are the Closing Skills for an IT Salesperson?

The ability to close deals and secure commitments from customers is essential for IT salespeople. Some key closing skills include:

1. **Asking for the sale:** IT salespeople should be comfortable and confident in asking for the sale, and be able to persuade the customer to make a purchase.
2. **Handling objections:** IT salespeople should be skilled at addressing and overcoming objections that customers may have about making a purchase.
3. **Negotiating terms:** IT salespeople should be able to negotiate the terms of the sale, including the price, payment terms, and any other details.
4. **Following up:** IT salespeople should follow up with customers after the sale to ensure their satisfaction, and address any questions or concerns they may have.

By developing these closing skills, IT salespeople can be more effective at securing commitments from customers and closing deals.

41 – Closing Mistakes

Here are some common sales closing mistakes to avoid:

1. Not understanding the customer's needs: Failing to understand the customer's needs and challenges can make it difficult to demonstrate how your product or service can help solve their problems.
2. Not addressing objections: Failing to anticipate or address objections or concerns that the prospect may have about your product or service can make it difficult to close the sale.
3. Being too aggressive: Being too aggressive or pushy can turn off the prospect and make them less likely to make a purchase. It's important to strike a balance

between persuading the prospect and respecting their decision-making process.
4. Failing to build rapport: Failing to build rapport with the prospect can make it difficult to establish a relationship and convince them to make a purchase.
5. Not using persuasive language: Failing to use persuasive language and techniques can make it difficult to convince the prospect that your product or service is the best solution for their needs.

By avoiding these mistakes, you can increase the likelihood of closing a sale and drive business growth.

Chapter 5

IT Domain Terminologies

1 – What Are the IT Business Terminologies?

Here are some common IT business terminologies:

1. **IT infrastructure:** the hardware, software, networks, and other components that make up an organization's IT system.
2. **Cloud computing:** the delivery of computing services, including servers, storage, databases, and software, over the internet.
3. **Cybersecurity:** the practice of protecting computer systems and networks from digital attacks, theft, and damage.
4. **Agile methodology:** a project management approach that emphasizes flexibility, collaboration, and rapid iterations.
5. **DevOps:** a set of practices that combines software development (Dev) and IT operations (Ops) to streamline and automate software delivery.

6. **Big data:** large, complex data sets that can be analyzed for insights and used to inform business decisions.
7. **Artificial intelligence (AI):** the simulation of human intelligence in machines, including tasks like problem-solving, speech recognition, and decision-making.
8. **Machine learning:** a type of AI that uses statistical algorithms to learn from data and improve over time.
9. **Internet of Things (IoT):** the network of physical devices, vehicles, appliances, and other objects embedded with sensors, software, and connectivity that allow them to exchange data and communicate with each other.
10. **Blockchain:** a decentralized digital ledger technology that records transactions in a secure and transparent way.

2 – What Are the IT Finance Terminologies?

Here are some common IT finance terminologies:

1. **Total Cost of Ownership (TCO):** the total cost of owning and operating an IT system over its lifetime, including initial purchase, maintenance, upgrades, and support.
2. **Return on Investment (ROI):** a measure of the financial return generated by an IT investment, calculated by dividing the net profit by the cost of the investment.

3. **Capital expenditure (CAPEX):** the upfront cost of acquiring a long-term asset, such as hardware or software, that will be used for several years.
4. **Operating expenditure (OPEX):** the ongoing cost of running an IT system, such as salaries, utilities, and maintenance.
5. **Depreciation:** the reduction in value of an IT asset over time, reflecting its diminishing usefulness and wear and tear.
6. **Amortization:** the process of spreading the cost of an intangible asset, such as software, over its useful life.
7. **Chargeback:** the practice of allocating IT costs to individual departments or users based on their usage or consumption of IT services.
8. **Budgeting:** the process of allocating financial resources for IT projects, based on organizational priorities and available funding.
9. **Financial analysis:** the use of financial data and metrics to assess the performance and viability of IT investments.
10. **Cost benefit analysis:** a method for evaluating the potential benefits and costs of an IT investment, to determine its overall value and return on investment.

3 – What Are the IT Technical Terminologies?

Here are some common IT technical terminologies:

1. **Algorithm:** a set of step-by-step instructions that a computer can follow to solve a problem or perform a task.
2. **Application programming interface (API):** a set of protocols, routines, and tools that developers use to build software applications.
3. **Backend:** the part of a software application or website that runs on a server and is not visible to the user.
4. **Code:** the programming instructions that tell a computer what to do.
5. **Database:** a collection of data organized in a way that allows for easy access, retrieval, and modification.
6. **Frontend:** the part of a software application or website that the user interacts with, including the user interface and visual design.
7. **Framework:** a set of tools, libraries, and conventions that developers use to build software applications more efficiently.
8. **Programming language:** a set of rules and syntax that developers use to write code, such as Java, Python, or C++.
9. **Server:** a computer system that provides resources or services to other computers on a network.
10. **Software development:** the process of designing, building, and testing software applications.
11. **User interface (UI):** the part of a software application or website that the user interacts with, including buttons, menus, and forms.
12. **Version control:** the practice of managing changes to software code over time, allowing multiple

developers to work on the same codebase without conflicts.

4 – What Are the IT Infrastructure Terminologies?

Here are some common IT infrastructure terminologies:

1. **Network:** a group of interconnected devices, such as computers, servers, routers, and switches, that can communicate and share data.
2. **Server:** a computer system that provides resources or services to other computers on a network, such as file storage, email, or web hosting.
3. **Router:** a device that connects different networks and routes data between them.
4. **Switch:** a device that connects devices within a network and allows them to communicate with each other.
5. **Firewall:** a software or hardware system that monitors and controls incoming and outgoing network traffic, to prevent unauthorized access or attacks.
6. **Virtualization:** the practice of creating a virtual version of a physical resource, such as a server or network, to maximize efficiency and flexibility.
7. **Cloud computing:** the delivery of computing services, including servers, storage, databases, and software, over the internet.

8. **Storage area network (SAN):** a specialized network that provides high-speed access to shared storage devices, such as disk arrays or tape libraries.
9. **Load balancer:** a device or software system that distributes incoming network traffic across multiple servers, to improve performance and reliability.
10. **Unified Communications (UC):** a set of communication and collaboration technologies, such as voice, video, messaging, and conferencing, that are integrated into a single system.

5 – What Are the IT Application Terminologies?

Here are some common IT application terminologies:

1. **Application:** a software program that performs a specific function, such as a word processor, spreadsheet, or database.
2. **Application server:** a server that provides the infrastructure and services required to run an application, such as web hosting or database access.
3. **Backend:** the part of an application or website that runs on a server and is not visible to the user.
4. **Bug:** an error or defect in an application that causes it to behave in unexpected ways or produce incorrect results.
5. **Debugging:** the process of identifying and fixing bugs in an application.

6. **Frontend:** the part of an application or website that the user interacts with, including the user interface and visual design.
7. **Graphical User Interface (GUI):** the visual components of an application or website that allow users to interact with it, such as buttons, menus, and forms.
8. **Middleware:** software that provides the communication and integration between different software applications or systems.
9. **Open source:** software that is distributed under an open-source license, allowing users to freely use, modify, and distribute it.
10. **Platform:** the underlying technology or infrastructure on which an application or software system runs, such as a specific operating system or cloud platform.
11. **Software development:** the process of designing, building, and testing software applications.
12. **User interface (UI):** the part of an application or website that the user interacts with, including buttons, menus, and forms.

6 – What Are the IT Managed Services Terminologies?

Here are some common IT managed services terminologies:

1. **IT service management (ITSM):** the practice of designing, delivering, managing, and improving IT

services to meet the needs of an organization and its customers.

2. **Service level agreement (SLA):** a contract between a service provider and a customer that specifies the level of service that will be provided, including performance metrics and guarantees.
3. **Help desk:** a service desk that provides technical support and assistance to end-users, typically via phone, email, or chat.
4. **Incident management:** the process of identifying, analyzing, and resolving IT incidents, such as system failures or security breaches.
5. **Problem management:** the process of identifying, analyzing, and resolving recurring IT problems to prevent them from happening again.
6. **Change management:** the process of planning, implementing, and monitoring changes to IT systems, applications, or processes to minimize disruption and maximize value.
7. **Network monitoring:** the process of continuously monitoring and analyzing network traffic and performance to identify and resolve issues.
8. **Patch management:** the process of managing and applying software patches and updates to keep IT systems secure and up-to-date.
9. **Backup and disaster recovery:** the process of creating and maintaining backups of IT systems and data to ensure business continuity in the event of a disaster or outage.
10. **Managed security services:** a set of security services, such as threat detection, vulnerability

management, and incident response, that are provided by a third-party provider to an organization.

7 – What Are the IT Consultancy Services Terminologies?

Here are some common IT consultancy services terminologies:

1. **IT strategy:** a plan for how an organization can use technology to achieve its business goals and objectives.
2. **Business process reengineering:** the process of analyzing and redesigning business processes to improve efficiency and effectiveness, often with the use of technology.
3. **IT assessment:** a process of evaluating an organization's IT systems and infrastructure to identify areas for improvement or optimization.
4. **IT audit:** a formal evaluation of an organization's IT systems, controls, and practices to ensure compliance with legal and regulatory requirements.
5. **IT governance:** the framework and processes used to manage IT resources and ensure they align with the organization's objectives.
6. **Digital transformation:** the use of technology to fundamentally change the way an organization operates, often with the goal of improving customer experience or creating new business models.
7. **IT project management:** the practice of planning, executing, and monitoring IT projects to ensure they

are delivered on time, within budget, and with the desired outcome.
8. **IT outsourcing:** the practice of hiring an external service provider to manage or operate some or all of an organization's IT systems and infrastructure.
9. **IT risk management:** the process of identifying, assessing, and mitigating risks related to an organization's IT systems and infrastructure.
10. **Vendor management:** the process of managing relationships with third-party vendors and service providers to ensure they deliver the required level of service and value.

8 – What Are the Cyber Security Terminologies?

Here are some common cyber security terminologies:

1. **Malware:** short for "malicious software," it refers to any software that is designed to harm a computer system or network, such as viruses, Trojans, and ransomware.
2. **Firewall:** a security system that monitors and controls incoming and outgoing network traffic based on predetermined security rules.
3. **Encryption:** the process of converting data into a coded format to protect it from unauthorized access.
4. **Cyberattack:** an attempt to gain unauthorized access to a computer system or network with the intent to steal, damage, or disrupt it.

5. **Phishing:** a social engineering attack in which an attacker uses email, phone, or other means to trick a user into disclosing sensitive information, such as login credentials or financial data.
6. **Two-factor authentication (2FA):** a security process that requires users to provide two forms of authentication, such as a password and a code sent to a mobile device, to access a system or application.
7. **Vulnerability:** a weakness or flaw in a computer system or network that can be exploited by an attacker to gain unauthorized access or perform other malicious actions.
8. **Intrusion detection system (IDS):** a security system that monitors network traffic for suspicious activity and alerts security personnel to potential threats.
9. **Penetration testing:** a security assessment in which ethical hackers attempt to exploit vulnerabilities in a system or network to identify weaknesses and improve security.
10. **Cybersecurity incident response:** the process of detecting, analyzing, and responding to cybersecurity incidents, such as data breaches or network intrusions, to minimize damage and prevent future incidents.

9 – What Are the IT Cloud Terminologies?

Here are some common IT cloud terminologies:

1. **Cloud computing:** the practice of using remote servers hosted on the Internet to store, manage, and

process data and applications, rather than using local servers or personal computers.
2. **Infrastructure as a service (IaaS):** a cloud computing service model in which a provider offers virtualized computing resources, such as servers and storage, to customers over the Internet.
3. **Platform as a service (PaaS):** a cloud computing service model in which a provider offers a platform for developing, deploying, and managing applications over the Internet, without the need for customers to manage underlying infrastructure.
4. **Software as a service (SaaS):** a cloud computing service model in which a provider offers applications over the Internet that are hosted and managed by the provider, rather than being installed on customers' computers or servers.
5. **Public cloud:** a cloud computing environment that is available to the general public and is hosted by a third-party provider, such as Amazon Web Services (AWS) or Microsoft Azure.
6. **Private cloud:** a cloud computing environment that is used exclusively by a single organization and is hosted either on-premises or by a third-party provider.
7. **Hybrid cloud:** a cloud computing environment that combines public and private cloud resources, allowing organizations to use a mix of on-premises and cloud-based resources.
8. **Cloud storage:** a service that allows users to store data in remote servers hosted by a third-party provider, typically accessed over the Internet.

9. **Cloud backup:** a service that allows users to automatically back up data from their computers or servers to remote servers hosted by a third-party provider.
10. **Cloud migration:** the process of moving data, applications, and other IT resources from on-premises infrastructure to a cloud computing environment.

10 – What Are the IT Business Continuity Terminologies?

Here are some common IT business continuity terminologies:

1. **Business continuity:** the ability of an organization to maintain essential functions during and after a disaster or disruptive event, such as a natural disaster, cyberattack, or equipment failure.
2. **Disaster recovery:** the process of recovering and restoring critical IT systems and infrastructure after a disaster or disruptive event.
3. **Recovery time objective (RTO):** the maximum amount of time it takes for an organization to recover and restore critical IT systems and infrastructure after a disaster or disruptive event.
4. **Recovery point objective (RPO):** the maximum amount of data loss that an organization can tolerate in the event of a disaster or disruptive event.
5. **Business continuity plan (BCP):** a comprehensive plan that outlines the steps an organization will take

to ensure business continuity in the event of a disaster or disruptive event.

6. **Risk assessment:** the process of identifying, assessing, and prioritizing potential risks and vulnerabilities that could impact an organization's ability to maintain business continuity.
7. **Continuity of operations plan (COOP):** a plan that outlines the steps an organization will take to ensure continuity of essential operations during a disruptive event.
8. **Hot site:** a fully equipped off-site facility that is designed to quickly and seamlessly take over critical IT functions in the event of a disaster or disruptive event.
9. **Cold site:** a backup facility that is not fully equipped but is available for use in the event of a disaster or disruptive event.
10. **Business impact analysis (BIA):** a process that assesses the potential impact of a disruptive event on an organization's operations, finances, and reputation, and helps prioritize business continuity planning efforts.

11 – What Are the IT NOC Terminologies?

Here are some common IT NOC (Network Operations Center) terminologies:

1. **Network operations center (NOC):** a central location where IT professionals monitor, maintain, and manage an organization's network infrastructure.

2. **Network monitoring:** the process of continuously monitoring network performance and activity to identify and resolve issues in real time.
3. **Incident management:** the process of managing and resolving incidents, or disruptions to normal network operation, in a timely and effective manner.
4. **Service level agreement (SLA):** a contract that specifies the level of service that a provider will deliver to a customer, including performance standards, response times, and other metrics.
5. **Network performance metrics:** key performance indicators (KPIs) used to measure the performance and health of network infrastructure, such as latency, throughput, and packet loss.
6. **Network topology:** the physical and logical layout of an organization's network infrastructure, including devices, connections, and protocols.
7. **Network security:** the set of practices and technologies used to protect network infrastructure and data from unauthorized access, attacks, and other threats.
8. **Network architecture:** the design and layout of an organization's network infrastructure, including hardware, software, and protocols.
9. **Ticketing system:** a system used to manage and track incidents, service requests, and other issues, often integrated with incident management and help desk software.
10. **Root cause analysis:** a process of identifying the underlying cause of an incident or problem, often

used to prevent future incidents or improve network performance

12 – What Are the IT SOC Terminologies?

Here are some common IT SOC (Security Operations Center) terminologies:

1. **Security operations center (SOC):** a central location where IT professionals monitor, analyze, and respond to security threats and incidents.
2. **Security information and event management (SIEM):** a software solution used to collect, aggregate, and analyze security event data from various sources, such as firewalls, intrusion detection systems, and antivirus software.
3. **Threat intelligence:** information about potential security threats, including sources, methods, and indicators of compromise.
4. **Vulnerability scanning:** the process of identifying and assessing vulnerabilities in an organization's network infrastructure and applications.
5. **Penetration testing:** a simulated attack on an organization's network infrastructure or applications to identify vulnerabilities and assess the effectiveness of security measures.
6. **Security incident and event management (SIEM):** the process of managing security events and incidents, including detection, analysis, response, and recovery.

7. **Security controls:** technical or administrative measures used to reduce the risk of security threats, such as access controls, encryption, and monitoring.
8. **Cyber threat intelligence (CTI):** a specialized type of threat intelligence that focuses on cyber threats, including malware, phishing, and hacking.
9. **Security posture:** an organization's overall level of security preparedness and resilience.
10. **Threat hunting:** the process of proactively searching for potential security threats and incidents in an organization's network infrastructure and applications.

13 – What Are the IT Data Centre Terminologies?

Here are some common IT Data Centre terminologies:

1. **Data center:** a facility used to house computer systems and associated components, such as telecommunications and storage systems.
2. **Rack:** a standardized frame used to mount multiple electronic equipment modules in a data center.
3. **Server:** a computer program or device that provides functionality to other devices or applications on a network.
4. **Virtualization:** the process of creating a virtual version of a resource, such as a server or network, to optimize usage and management.

5. **Cloud computing:** the delivery of computing services over the internet, including servers, storage, databases, and software.
6. **Backup and recovery:** the process of creating and storing copies of data to protect against data loss and facilitate recovery in the event of a disaster or system failure.
7. **Power distribution unit (PDU):** a device used to distribute electrical power within a data center.
8. **Cooling systems:** equipment used to control the temperature and humidity within a data center to prevent equipment overheating and failure.
9. **Colocation:** the practice of housing multiple customers' equipment in a single data center facility.
10. **Uptime:** the percentage of time that a system or service is available and operational.

14 – What Are the IT DR Terminologies?

Here are some common IT DR (Disaster Recovery) terminologies:

1. **Disaster recovery (DR):** a process of restoring critical IT systems and data in the event of a disaster, such as a natural disaster, cyber-attack, or hardware failure.
2. **Recovery time objective (RTO):** the maximum amount of time it should take to restore an IT system after a disaster.

3. **Recovery point objective (RPO):** the maximum amount of data loss that is acceptable in the event of a disaster.
4. **Business continuity planning (BCP):** the process of creating a plan to ensure that critical business functions can continue in the event of a disaster.
5. **High availability (HA):** a system or application designed to minimize downtime and ensure continuous operation.
6. **Redundancy:** the use of backup systems, components, or processes to minimize the impact of a failure or disruption.
7. **Failover:** the process of automatically switching to a backup system or component in the event of a failure or disruption.
8. **Replication:** the process of copying data from one location to another to ensure availability and prevent data loss.
9. **Hot site:** a disaster recovery site that is always ready to take over operations in the event of a disaster.
10. **Cold site:** a disaster recovery site that is not operational until a disaster occurs.

15 – What Are the IT Production site Terminologies?

Here are some common IT Production Site terminologies
1. **Production site:** a location where a company's IT systems and applications are deployed and used to support the organization's core business operations.

2. **Service level agreement (SLA):** a contract between a service provider and a customer that defines the level of service expected, including availability, response times, and other metrics.
3. **Capacity planning:** the process of determining the computing resources required to meet anticipated demand for IT services.
4. **Load balancing:** the process of distributing network traffic across multiple servers or systems to optimize performance and prevent overloading.
5. **High availability (HA):** a system or application designed to minimize downtime and ensure continuous operation.
6. **Scalability:** the ability of a system or application to handle increasing levels of demand without a decrease in performance.
7. **Disaster recovery (DR):** a process of restoring critical IT systems and data in the event of a disaster, such as a natural disaster, cyber-attack, or hardware failure.
8. **Change management:** the process of planning, testing, and implementing changes to IT systems and applications to minimize the risk of disruption.
9. **DevOps:** a methodology that emphasizes collaboration and communication between development and operations teams to optimize the delivery and maintenance of IT services.
10. **Incident management:** the process of managing and resolving IT incidents, including communication with stakeholders and documentation of the incident and response.

16 – What Are the IT HCI Terminologies?

Here are some common IT HCI (Hyperconverged Infrastructure) terminologies:

1. **Hyperconverged Infrastructure (HCI):** a software-defined infrastructure that combines compute, storage, and networking in a single system, managed by a single interface.
2. **Virtualization:** the process of creating a virtual version of a physical resource, such as a server, storage device, or network.
3. **Software-defined:** a term used to describe IT infrastructure that is managed and controlled by software rather than hardware.
4. **Cluster:** a group of interconnected servers or nodes that work together to provide computing resources and services.
5. **Node:** a single physical server in a cluster that provides compute, storage, and networking resources.
6. **Scale-out:** the ability to add more nodes to a cluster to increase computing resources and capacity.
7. **Scale-up:** the ability to add more resources, such as CPU or RAM, to a single node to increase computing power.
8. **Data locality:** the ability to store data on the same node or server that is running the application that needs the data, reducing latency and improving performance.

9. **Deduplication:** the process of identifying and eliminating duplicate data to save storage space and improve efficiency.
10. **Compression:** the process of reducing the size of data to save storage space and improve efficiency.

17 – What Are the IT Storage Terminologies?

Here are some common IT storage terminologies:

1. **Storage Area Network (SAN):** a dedicated, high-speed network that provides access to block-level storage devices, such as disk arrays, for multiple servers.
2. **Network Attached Storage (NAS):** a file-level storage technology that provides file-level access to shared storage devices over a network.
3. **Direct Attached Storage (DAS):** a storage device that is directly attached to a single server or computer.
4. **RAID:** Redundant Array of Independent Disks, a technology that combines multiple hard disks into a single logical unit to improve performance, reliability, or both.
5. **LUN:** Logical Unit Number, a unique identifier assigned to a logical unit, which is a portion of a physical disk drive that is presented to the host as a separate storage device.
6. **Storage Virtualization:** a technique that abstracts physical storage resources into logical storage pools, enabling greater flexibility and management.

7. **Backup:** the process of creating a copy of data in case the original data is lost or damaged.
8. **Archiving:** the process of moving data that is no longer actively used to a separate storage device for long-term retention.
9. **Tiered Storage:** a strategy that uses different types of storage media, such as solid-state drives (SSDs) and hard disk drives (HDDs), to optimize performance and cost.
10. **Storage Management:** the process of managing storage devices and resources to ensure data is available, accessible, and protected.

18 – What Are the IT Compute Terminologies?

Here are some common IT compute terminologies:

1. **CPU:** Central Processing Unit, the primary processing unit in a computer that carries out instructions of a computer program.
2. **Processor:** a chip that contains one or more CPUs, and can perform tasks such as arithmetic, logical, and input/output operations.
3. **Clock Speed:** the rate at which a processor executes instructions, measured in gigahertz (GHz).
4. **Cores:** the number of independent processing units in a CPU, which can perform tasks simultaneously.
5. **Thread:** a sequence of instructions that can be executed independently by a CPU, which can

improve performance by executing multiple tasks at the same time.
6. **Memory:** a component in a computer that stores data and program instructions for the CPU to access quickly.
7. **RAM:** Random Access Memory, a type of memory that allows data to be read and written quickly, but is volatile and loses data when power is turned off.
8. **Cache:** a type of memory that is used to store frequently accessed data or instructions for faster access.
9. **Virtualization:** the process of creating a virtual version of a physical resource, such as a server, storage device, or network.
10. **High-Performance Computing (HPC):** a type of computing that uses supercomputers and parallel processing techniques to perform complex computations quickly and efficiently.

19 – What Are the IT AI Terminologies?

Here are some common IT AI (Artificial Intelligence) terminologies:

1. **Machine Learning:** a type of AI that enables computers to learn and improve from experience without being explicitly programmed.
2. **Deep Learning:** a subset of machine learning that uses artificial neural networks with multiple layers to analyze complex data sets.

3. **Neural Network:** a system of interconnected artificial neurons that work together to solve complex problems.
4. **Natural Language Processing (NLP):** a branch of AI that enables computers to understand, interpret, and generate human language.
5. **Computer Vision:** a branch of AI that enables computers to interpret and understand visual information from the world.
6. **Reinforcement Learning:** a type of machine learning that uses trial and error to learn through reward-based systems.
7. **Chatbot:** a computer program that uses natural language processing to simulate human conversation, often used for customer service or support.
8. **Speech Recognition:** a technology that enables computers to recognize and interpret spoken language.
9. **Image Recognition:** a technology that enables computers to identify objects, people, or patterns in images.
10. **AI Model:** a mathematical representation of an AI system that is used to make predictions, generate insights, or solve complex problems.

20 – What Are the IT BI Terminologies?

Here are some common IT BI (Business Intelligence) terminologies:

1. **Data Warehouse:** a centralized repository that stores data from various sources and is used for reporting and analysis.
2. **ETL:** Extract, Transform, and Load, a process for moving data from various sources into a data warehouse.
3. **OLAP:** Online Analytical Processing, a technology that enables multidimensional analysis of data.
4. **Data Mart:** a subset of a data warehouse that is designed for a specific business unit or department.
5. **Dimension:** a characteristic of data that is used for analysis, such as time, geography, or product.
6. **Measure:** a numeric value that is used for analysis, such as revenue, profit, or quantity.
7. **Dashboard:** a visual representation of key performance indicators (KPIs) and metrics that provides insights into business performance.
8. **Scorecard:** a tool for monitoring and measuring progress towards business goals and objectives.
9. **Data Mining:** the process of extracting patterns and insights from large data sets.
10. **Self-Service BI:** a type of BI that enables business users to access and analyze data without the assistance of IT or data analysts.

21 – What Are the IT Support Service Terminologies?

Here are some common IT support service terminologies:

1. **Service Desk:** a single point of contact for users to report issues, request assistance, or make inquiries about IT services.
2. **Incident Management:** a process for managing and resolving incidents or service disruptions.
3. **Problem Management:** a process for identifying and addressing the root causes of recurring incidents.
4. **Change Management:** a process for managing changes to IT infrastructure, applications, or services to minimize the risk of disruption.
5. **Request Fulfillment:** a process for fulfilling user requests for IT services or resources.
6. **SLA:** Service Level Agreement, a document that outlines the expected level of service for an IT service or application.
7. **ITIL:** Information Technology Infrastructure Library, a framework for managing IT services and processes.
8. **Remote Support:** providing IT support services to users remotely, often using remote access tools.
9. **On-site Support:** providing IT support services to users in person at their location.
10. **Escalation:** the process of escalating an issue or request to a higher level of support or management.

22 – What Are the IT Network Terminologies?

Here are some common IT network terminologies:

1. **Network:** A group of interconnected devices that can communicate with each other.
2. **LAN (Local Area Network):** A network that covers a small geographic area, such as a single office building or campus.
3. **WAN (Wide Area Network):** A network that covers a large geographic area, such as a city or multiple cities.
4. **Router:** A device that connects multiple networks together and routes data packets between them.
5. **Switch:** A device that connects multiple devices within a single network and forwards data packets to their intended destination.
6. **Firewall:** A device or software program that helps to protect a network by filtering incoming and outgoing traffic based on a set of rules.
7. **IP Address:** A unique numerical identifier assigned to each device on a network.
8. **DNS (Domain Name System):** A system that translates domain names into IP addresses.
9. **DHCP (Dynamic Host Configuration Protocol):** A protocol that automatically assigns IP addresses to devices on a network.
10. **Gateway:** A device that connects a network to the Internet.
11. **Protocol:** A set of rules governing communication between devices on a network.
12. **TCP/IP (Transmission Control Protocol/Internet Protocol):** A set of protocols used for communication between devices on the Internet.

13. **VLAN (Virtual Local Area Network):** A logical network that groups devices together based on factors such as location, function, or department.
14. **VPN (Virtual Private Network):** A secure connection between two networks that allows remote users to access resources as if they were directly connected to the network.